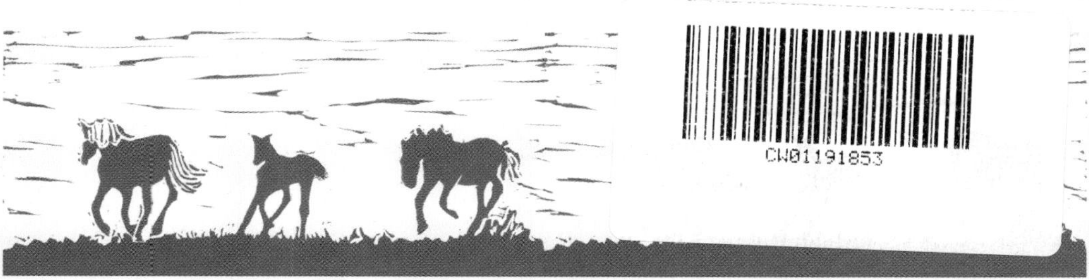



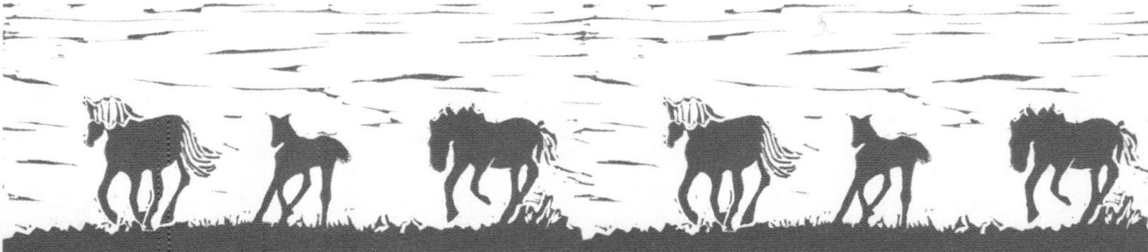

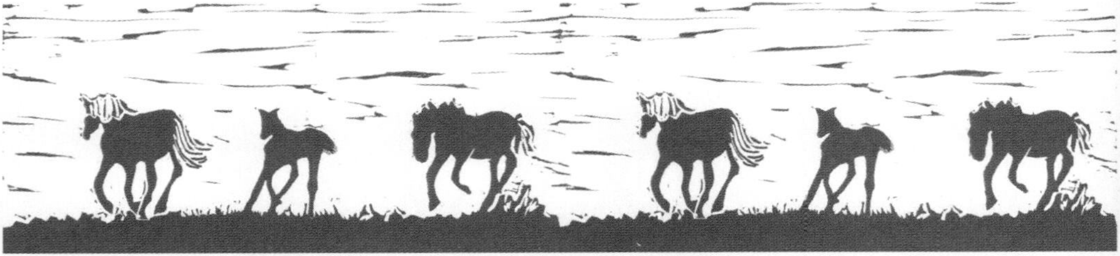

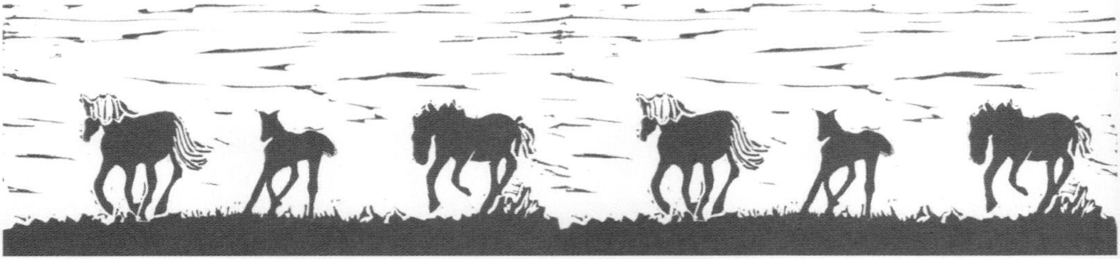

# The Native Pony Book

by Jane Russ

**GRAFFEG**

## Dedication

In memory of my two best equine chums, Teddy Roosevelt and Absolutely Crackers. I learnt as much from them as they learnt from me and I am very grateful to have had their companionships.

# Contents

| | |
|---|---|
| 5 | Introduction |
| 9 | Carneddau Pony |
| 19 | Connemara Pony |
| 27 | Dales Pony |
| 39 | Dartmoor Pony |
| 49 | Eriskay Pony |
| 57 | Exmoor Pony |
| 71 | Fell Pony |
| 83 | Highland Pony |
| 97 | Kerry Bog Pony |
| 105 | New Forest Pony |
| 117 | Shetland Pony |
| 129 | Welsh Mountain Pony |
| 142 | The Rare Breeds Survival Trust |
| 145 | Myth and Legend |
| 153 | Art and Literature |
| 159 | Photo credits and artworks |
| 160 | Acknowledgements |

Fell Ponies

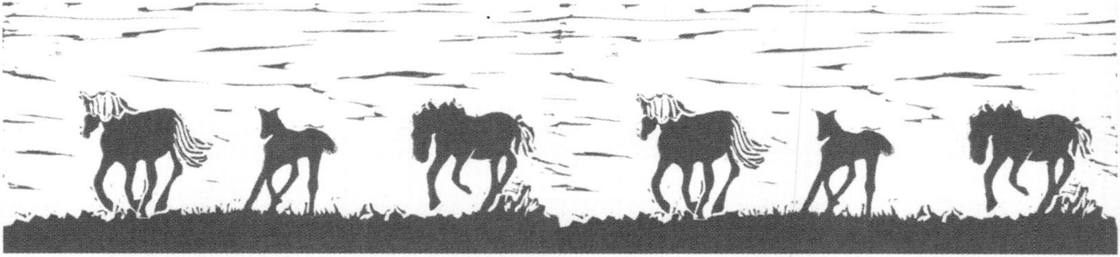

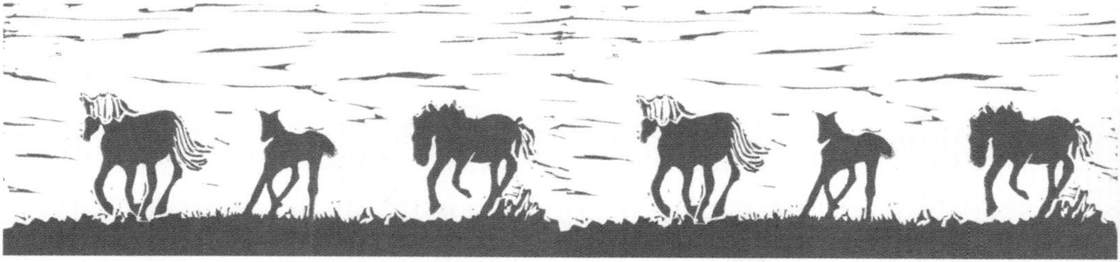

# Books in the series

| | | |
|---|---|---|
| The Hare Book | The Fox Book | The Owl Book |
| The Red Squirrel Book | The Bee Book | The Robin Book |
| The Hedgehog Book | The Badger Book | The Puffin Book |

www.graffeg.com

# Introduction

In 1961 I received *The Observer's Book of Horses & Ponies* as a birthday present. I still have it, inscribed 'To Jane from Aunty Dolly' – that Dolly; I was only nine but she really knew where my heart lay. It has gone into family legend how, aged three, I dragged my mother across the road to press my face against the railings and watch the pony pulling the lawn mower in the park. He was wearing leather boots to protect the grass and I was fascinated by him. We had to go directly to the greengrocers to get a carrot for the pony and I was head over heals in love from that first horse-scented crunch.

By the time I started riding lessons at seven we lived in Plymouth and the lessons took place on Dartmoor. Not near Dartmoor but actually on the moor. I lived for my Saturday pony fix and would cry for hours if it was cancelled because of inclement weather. Using my identification book I learnt how to recognise all the major horse and pony breeds and, this being 1961, every day out was accompanied by the *I-Spy Horses and Ponies* book too.

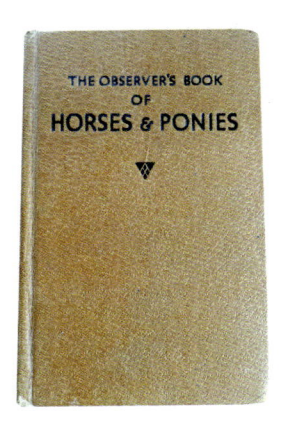

The idea for this book came to me when I found my Observer's Book again last year and started thinking about those native breeds I had taken for granted in the late 50s and wondering if they were still there for me to show my grandchildren. There has been talk in the media about moorland and woodland ponies causing traffic incidents and the more I looked into where the native pony nation was now, the more convinced I became that it was time for me to catch up with my first love.

In this book I have tried to illustrate the breeds as they are meant to be seen, not clean and perfect in the show ring but out against a natural backdrop. Where they exist, I have also mentioned any current uses for these ponies logging, ghillieing, even as pack ponies. It has been a joy to write and proved that Aunty Dolly knew me really well when she gave me that book back in 1961.

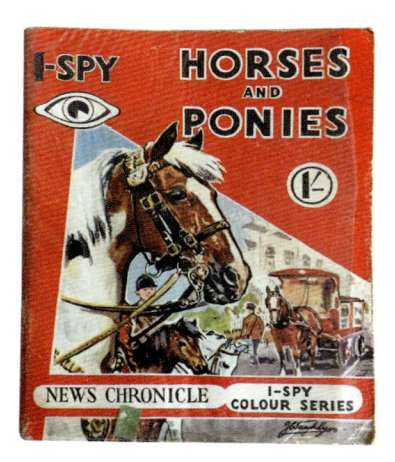

The author with Laddie

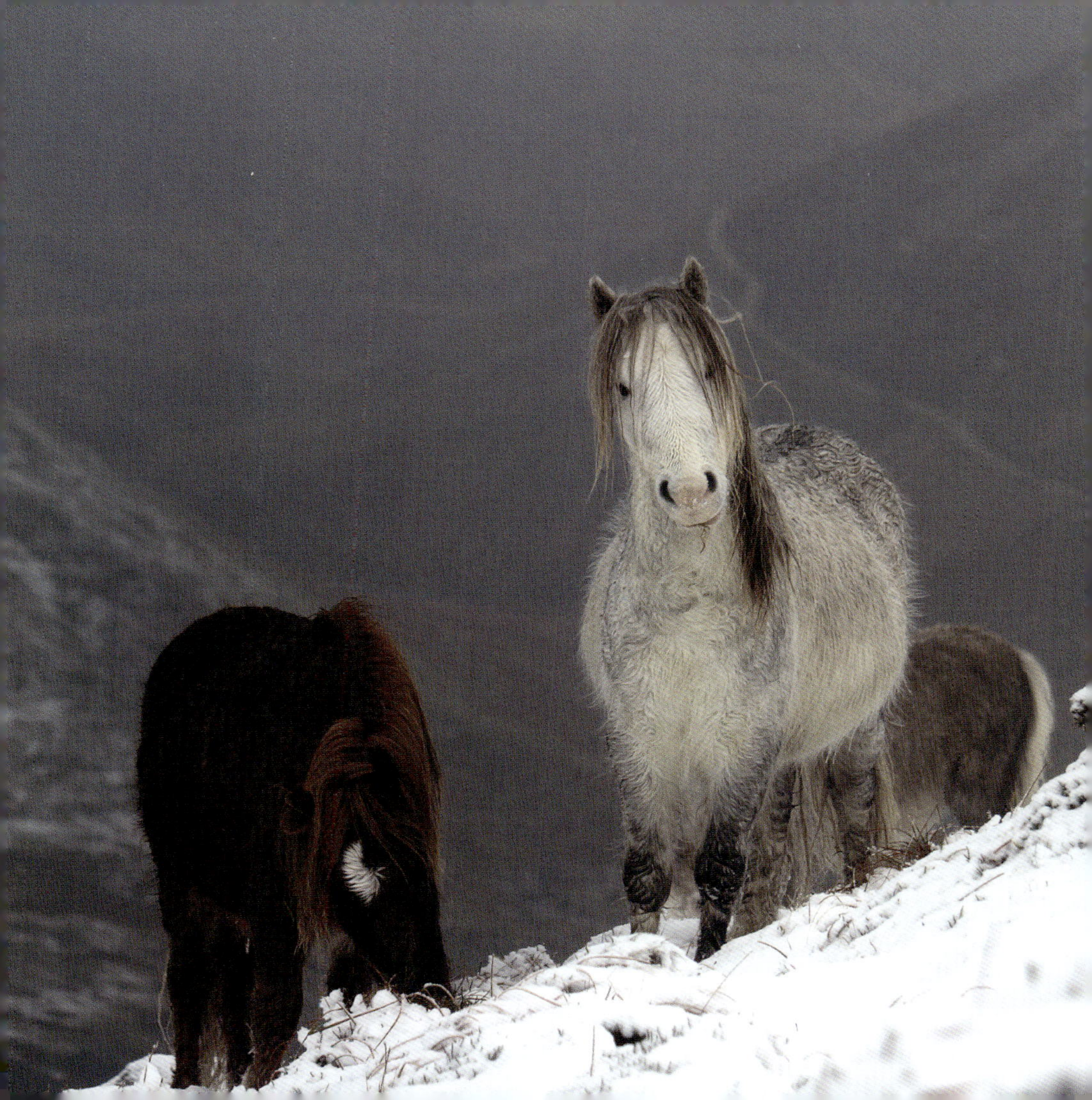

Carneddau Stallions

# Carneddau Pony

It is probable that even those who take an interest in native ponies may never have heard of the UK's oldest breed, the Carneddau pony (pronounced car-neth-eye). These feral ponies roam the deeply inhospitable north Wales mountain range for which they are named. The terrain covers around 200 square kilometers of the Snowdonia National Park and includes cliffs and rocky slopes, bogs, lakes, and mountains up to 3,000 feet high. It is estimated that the Carneddau ponies have been running these mountains since the Bronze age. Recent archaeological evidence indicates that the first axe heads in the UK were made in the Llanfairfechan area and it seems possible that the ponies were used transporting them to the rest of the country and even to Brittany.

**Carneddau Pony Society**
See Carneddau ponies on Twitter and FaceBook.

**Height:** 10hh –11hh*.

**Colours:** grey, black, brown, bay, dun (the original colour), roan, chestnut and palomino, both dark and blue-eyed cream.

**Characteristics as described by Carneddau Pony Society:** Semi-feral with a sturdy solid body, a thick layered warm and waterproof coat and dainty hair-filled ears. Strong and determined in nature, their small size belies a big warm-hearted personality.

**Status:** Not yet designated a rare breed: there are only approximately 220 breeding mares on the Carneddau range in the Snowdonia National Park.

*hands high is a unique measurement for horses. One hand is equal to 4 inches (10 cm).

It is often stated that in ACT 32 HEN. VIII (1541), Henry VIII ordered all ponies in the country to be destroyed because they were too small to carry a knight in a suit of armour. This is not quite the case. In fact it was about the use of common land. What the Act actually ordered was the use of 'drifts' or the annual herding of ponies from land held in common between farmers and tenants, to cull out the old, the infirm and check that any mares/stallions would be likely to produce foals of a 'reasonable stature'. No height restriction is mentioned and the selection was at the discretion of those responsible for the drift (often a small group of local farmers and or tenants). One could imagine, bearing in mind there would be no compensation for animals destroyed, the drift drivers would only cull those ponies that were patently below standard.

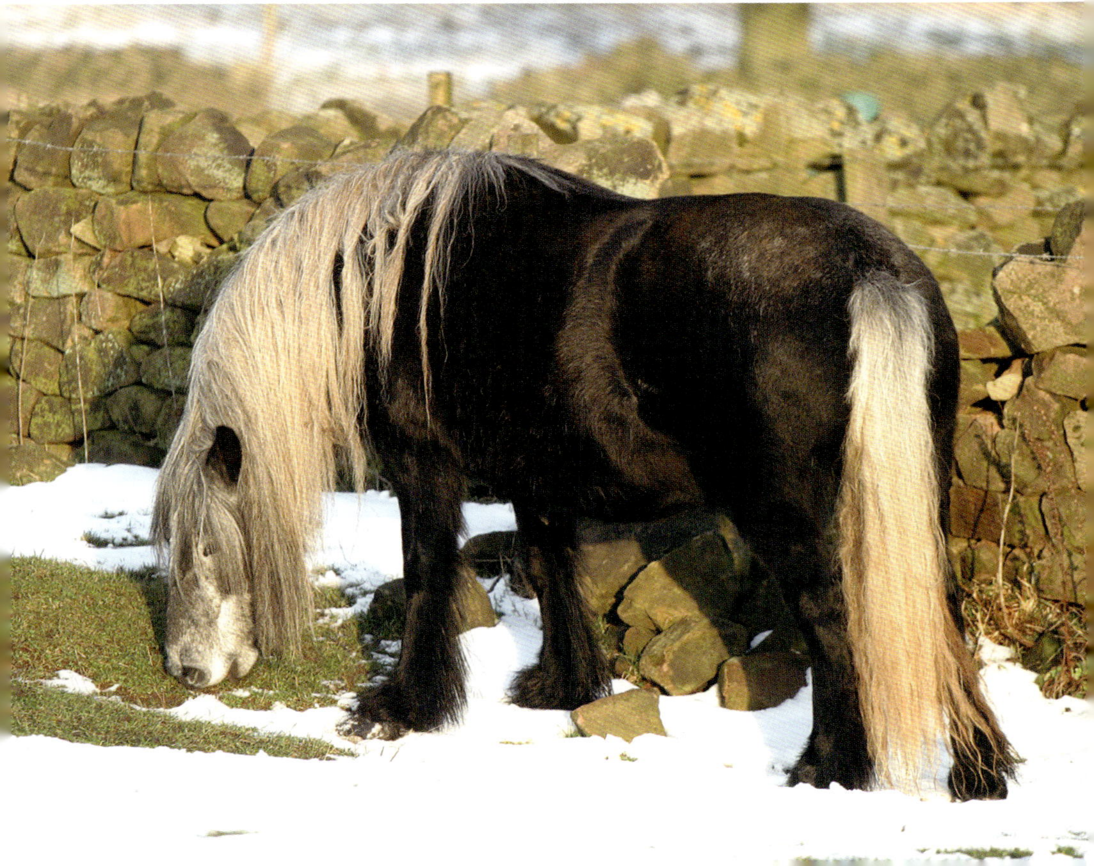

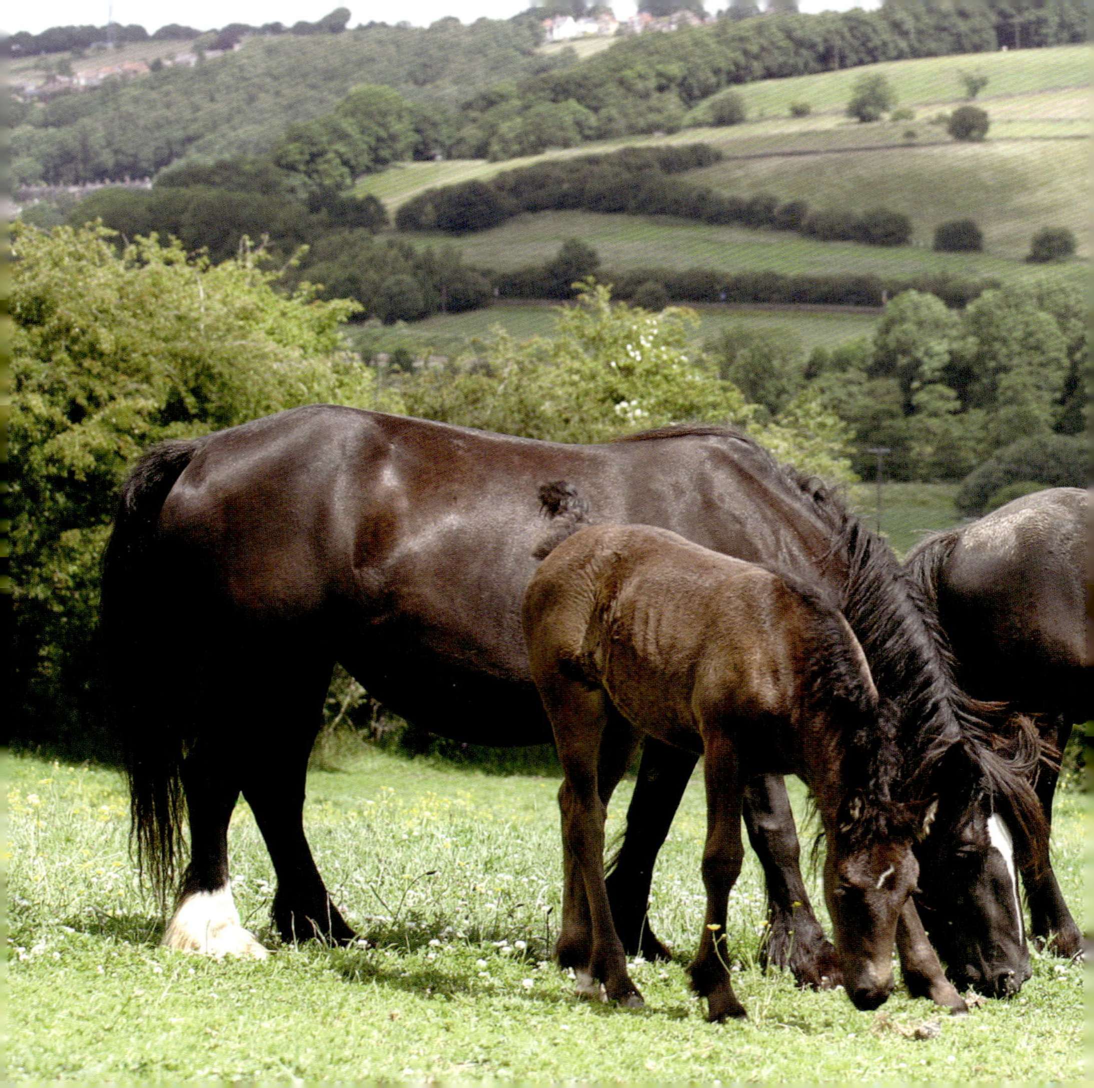

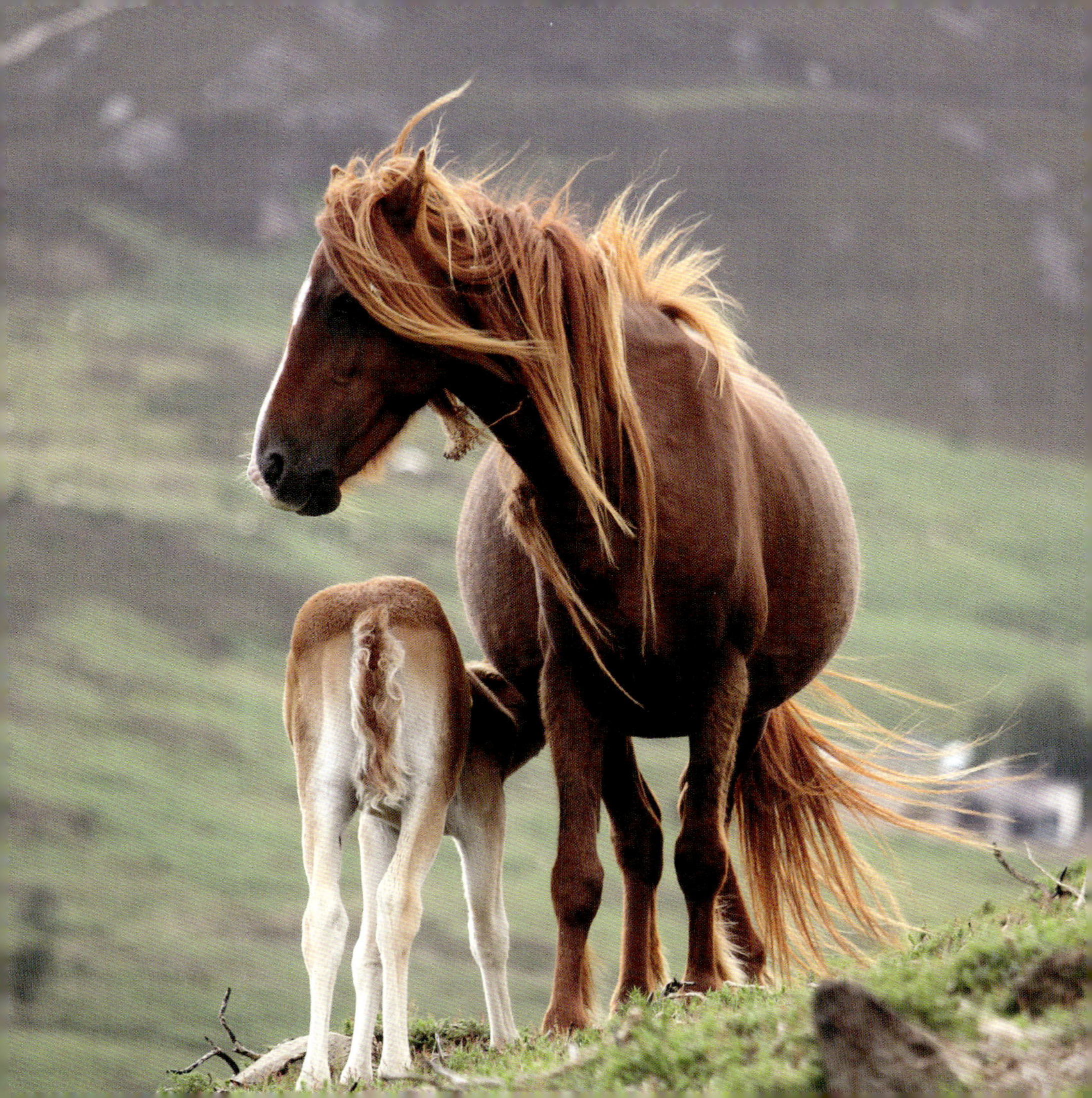

Furthermore, the Act presupposed that inaccessible mountains and hills would be able to have a drift, which of course in many cases they could not.

Ponies during this period had many uses within a community; in the fields, for transport, and for commerce. Subsequently however, as much as Henry may have wanted to thin out the pony population, this did not happen. By the time of the Civil War (1642), the average height of ponies, apart from those specifically bred in enclosures and often from imported stock lines, is well documented at about thirteen hands.

The Carneddau are supremely surefooted and have thick layered waterproof coats and small fur-filled ears, both of which help them cope with whatever the mountains throw at them. Timing unfortunately is everything and in March 2013 a snowstorm on the Carneddau killed approximately 100 ponies. Unfortunately, amongst the dead were many mares about to drop foals, so both mare and foal were lost to the herd. In the nature of a truly ecological end, apart from those on or near footpaths, the carcasses were left on the mountain to feed foxes and other carrion eaters. This was natural selection at its most raw, perhaps a perfect example of survival of the fittest.

For centuries the Carneddau have adapted to survive, living as nature intended, far from the more sheltered lives of most ponies in the UK today. In the mid-1970s someone tried turning some Welsh Section A ponies out on the mountain. These are the Welsh Mountain ponies closest in size and type to the Carneddau. Sadly, none of them survived; even they were not equipped to cope with life on the hills.

The ponies have run the mountains under the stewardship of local farmers and landowners for at least 370 years, which is when records began. 1967 saw the registration of each farm that wanted grazing rights for ponies and sheep. The right to graze goes with the farm itself but this right can be leased to a third party. There are currently seven farms entitled to do this.

Before the instigation of registration, the ponies had ear 'nicks' to show to whom they belonged. These would be used to sort the animals when they were driven down off the mountain in the annual 'drift' in November. Ear nicks were superseded by ear tags and now microchips. The Setiwr is the 'policeman' of the mountain who can be called upon to mitigate in disputes of ownership. Every parish has their own setiwr. In 2006 the EU gave a grant to the area which resulted in sheep being taken off the mountain and the formal setting up of The Carneddau Pony Society (CPS). Following pressure from the CPS, the Welsh Sennedd designated the Carneddau a breed and thus gave them the right to be microchipped, therefore ensuring they could be exported if a buyer lived abroad.

At the annual drift youngsters, mainly males, are removed from their herds and re-homed, with many going to what has become a new and

The Native Pony Book

crucial purchaser in the context of enviornmental conservation. The UK is gradually realising the importance of conservation grazing across mountain and moorland and, like other native breeds, the Carneddau is playing an important role in this. At the time of a drift, surplus ponies will be offered for sale. Pori, Natur a Threftadaeth (PONT), is the grazing organisation of Wales and they work with other groups such as local councils, RSPB, and farmers to find areas that need ponies for conservation grazing. The hardiness, sure-footedness and feral nature of the Carneddau make them perfect to oversee areas unsuitable for cattle or where cattle are not appropriate such as areas with a high incidence of bovine TB. PONT considers itself part of a circular ecology, supporting both the continuation of the breed and the Welsh environment in which it lives.

These approximately 200 wild ponies are not yet designated as a rare breed. Despite this they have been genetically proven by Dr. Debbie Nash at Aberystwyth University to have a unique DNA. At some point in their very distant past they may have had a link to the more familiar Welsh Section A pony but their genetic signature shows that they have lived in isolation for at least several hundred years. The Carneddau has not had its existence 'managed' in any sense; they have lived alone on their mountain with minimal human contact, having a symbiotic relationship with the land and it with them. Professor Susanne

Shultz of Manchester University has been studying the social groupings for many years and has found that these herds form the backbone of the hillside pony community. Interestingly, she has discovered that stress in the 'drift' does not come on descending the mountain when being gathered but instead occurs on release, when ponies try to find their fellow herd members.

The Carneddau ponies survive in an inhospitable landscape but it is their very wildness that supports this survival. Long may they continue.

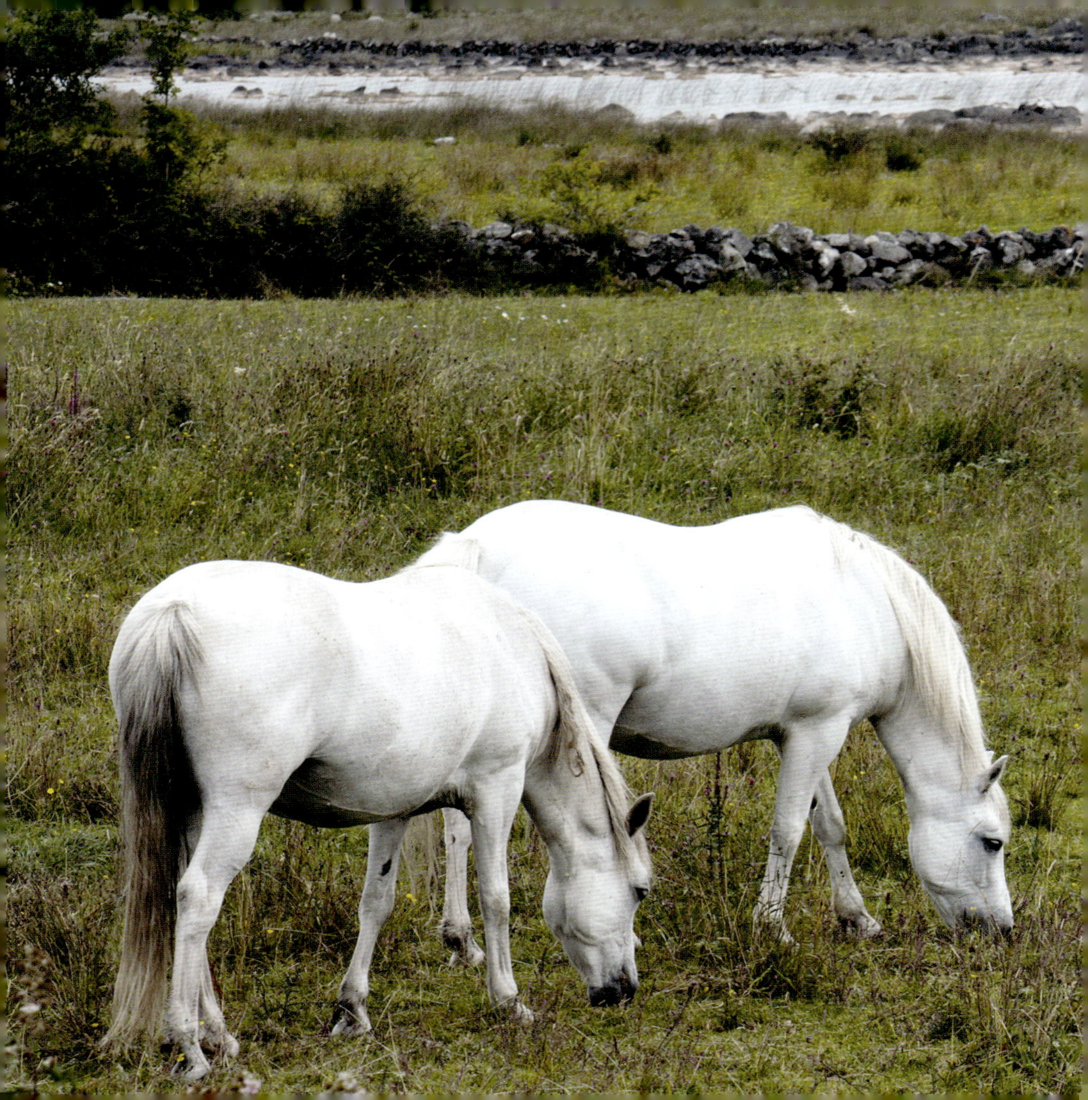

# Connemara Pony

The natural home of the Connemara pony is Connaught in Ireland, west of Lough Corrib and Lough Mask. This area, with the Atlantic Ocean to the west and Galway Bay to the south, is a larger district than that actually called Connemara in general parlance.

The only truly indigenous pony of Ireland, the Connemara has lived an almost feral life in a rugged landscape of peatbogs, moors, hills and the seastrand. It has fed mainly on grass, herbs, sedges and rushes. These feedstuffs, because of the microclimate of the Gulf Stream, are available to eat early in the year. The ponies will also take seaweed when grazing right beside the sea, giving them added vitamins and minerals. It is worth noting that, like many native breeds normally raised on 'poor' grazing, the Connemara has

**British Connemara Pony Society**
www.britishconnemaras.co.uk

**Height:** 13hh–15hh*.

**Colours:** grey, black, brown, bay, dun (the original colour), roan, chestnut and palomino, both dark and blue-eyed cream.

**Characteristics as described by the British Connemara Pony Society:** Good temperament, hardiness and staying power, intelligence, soundness, sure-footedness, jumping ability, suitable for child or adult. Movement is free, easy and true, without undue knee action but active and covering the ground.

*hands high is a unique measurement for horses. One hand is equal to 4 inches (10 cm).

a predisposition to get fat on a rich stable diet and subsequently develop laminitis, an extremely painful condition of the feet linked to being overweight.

Perhaps the most ancient of the native breeds, the origins of the Connemara are often disputed and have not been proven. Did the Celts bring horses with them in the 4th century BC when they came to our islands from the Alps, through Spain and Gaul? They are known to have been good horsemen so perhaps they did. When the Spanish Armada ran aground in 1588, were horses saved from the sea and did they breed with the Irish stock? The Armada certainly happened so it is possible. Did Spanish horses in fact come to Ireland not via the Armada but through Galway City, brought in by merchants wanting to enhance their personal status? No-one can confirm these hypotheses but it is not disputed that the Connemara is a very ancient breed.

In 1897, the Connemara was described to the Irish Commission on Horse Breeding as 'an extremely hardy, wiry class of pony, showing a great deal of the Barb or Arab blood... good shoulders, good hard legs, good action and great stamina.' However, it was also noted that the influence of the Arab and Barb was deteriorating with the passage of time. This deterioration was not helped by the practice of turning any old stallion out on the hills to cover mares and thus weakening the calibre of the stock.

Eventually Welsh stallions were brought across to help raise the quality and in 1904 the legendary stallion Cannon Ball was foaled. (He subsequently was the first stallion in The Connemara Pony Breeders

Society stud book published in 1926.) However, this importation of stallions was not the real answer and in 1901 Professor J. C. Ewart of Edinburgh University, completed a report following a study he made into horse breeding in this region of Ireland in conjunction with local experts. He made three suggestions for the betterment and longevity of the breed, as he considered it most important not to breed out the natural hardiness, strength, stamina and temperament.

i) the best Connemara stallions should be bought

ii) a register of the best purebred mares be created

iii) local farmers be encouraged to be more selective about the stallions allowed to run on the mountains

Finally, in 1923, The Connemara Pony Breeders Society (CPBS) came into being followed by inspections of ponies in 1924 and 1925. By 1939, the CPBS, who managed the covering of mares by approved stallions, owned ten of the fourteen stallions. Owners were notified in Volume IV of the stud book that inspections for registrations would be carried out at Annual Shows and at twenty-five local centres. The plan worked and the Connemara today has antecedence that can be followed back through clearly defined breed lines.

Breeders often speak of the versatility of the Connemara, the way it is a perfect one-size-fits-all family pony if you are a child, an adult, need to hack out occasionally or compete at Pony Club or eventing. Provided it fits you for size, the Connie will be there for you. The strength and natural agility of this native breed cannot be underestimated and one cannot talk of Connemara ponies without mentioning their outstanding ability in show jumping. One, called Nugget, cleared a 7' 2" puissance wall at the Olympia Horse Show in 1935 to say nothing of the outstanding Connemara/Thoroughbred Stroller and his rider, Marion Coakes. Stroller at 14.1hh, won 61 international show jumping competitions, including a silver medal at the 1968 Mexico Olympics.

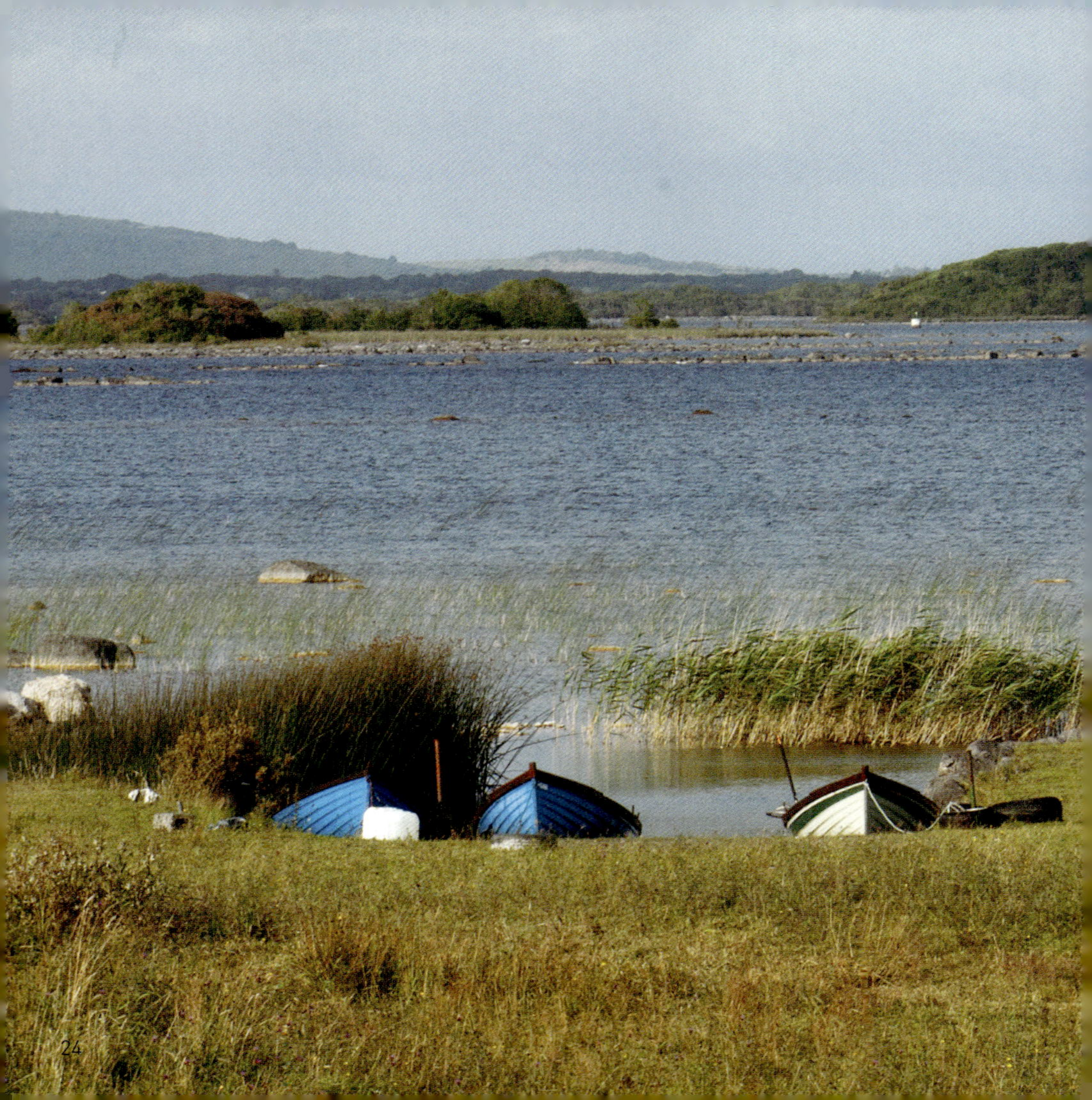

The orderly movement of such large loads (approximately 100kg carried in two panniers on either side of the pony) was down to the powerful qualities of the Galloway pony. Over such long distances, perhaps as much as 240 miles per week, it can only be imagined what chaos could have ensued with a less capable, less strong animal. Once they reached their coastal destination they might be reloaded with wood or coal to carry back to base to keep the smelting fires stoked.

Eventually mining ponies were superseded by the steam engine and the motor car, and the ponies spread out from the pits and were utilised elsewhere, with the last set of pack ponies being auctioned in 1879. The first Dales pony showing class had been held ten years before in 1869. Gradually the pit and pack ponies were brought onto farms and small holdings in the area, where canny farmers ran them with the Dales ponies they had running on the hills already. The original Galloways from Scotland subsequently became extinct but the crossbreeds eventually became the Dales ponies we know today.

Common grazing was available in the past and ponies would be turned out on the hills; not so today however, where all land in this area is in ownership. 'Fields' may be 80 acres but it does mean there are no truly wild Dales ponies.

One unusual fact about Dales ponies is that they were well beloved of country butchers, who had long rounds in varied countryside. They sold meat but they also bought cattle 'on the hoof' and would be

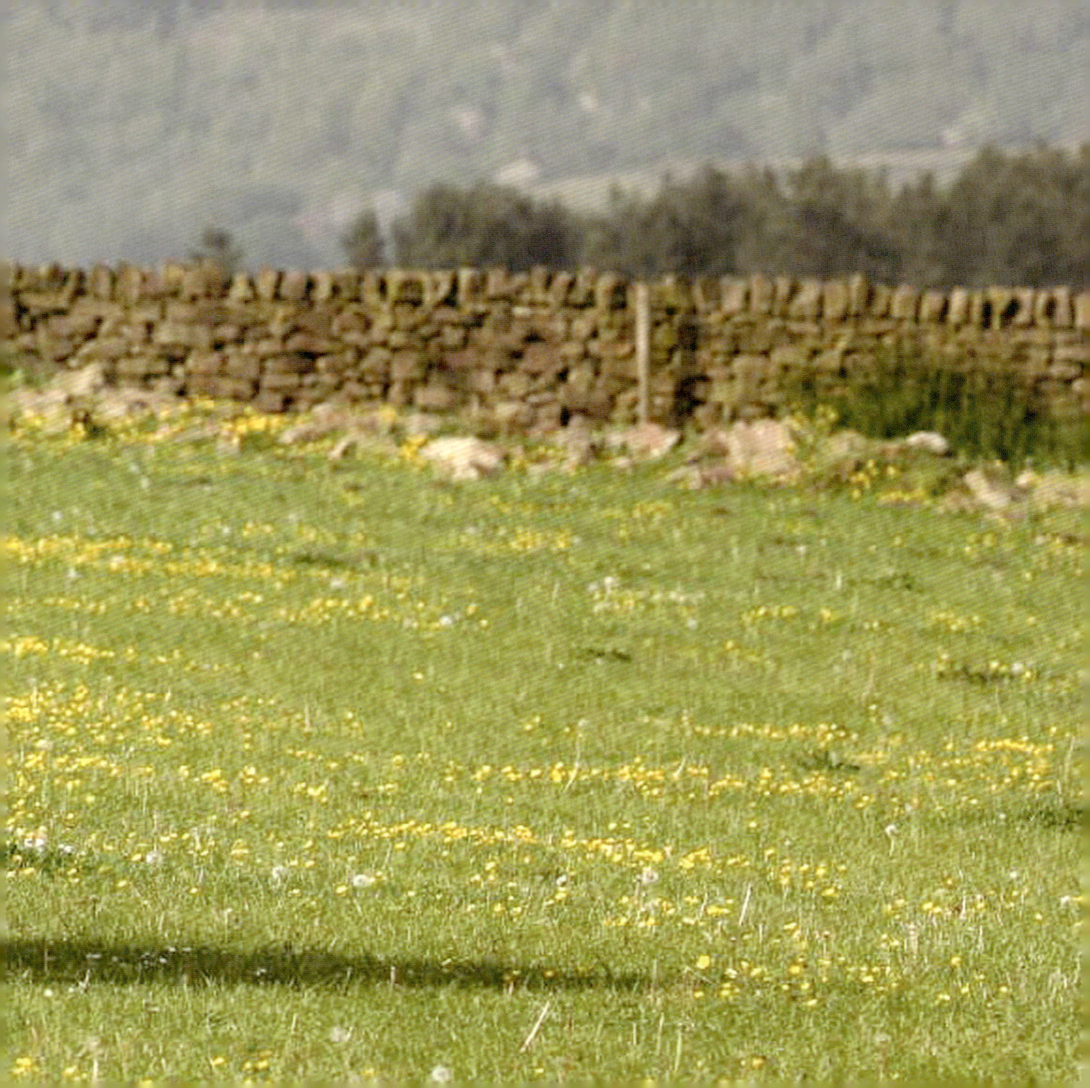

# The Dales pony was much valued by the Army during the First World War, where its natural strength, stamina and intelligence played an important part in the heat of battle.

The Dales pony was much valued by the Army during the First World War, where its natural strength, stamina and intelligence played an important part in the heat of battle. Farmers also found the Dales to be just the all-rounder they needed; good behind a plough and in the shafts of a farm cart, suitable as they say, to 'ride and drive'. Small tenant farmers with a family could cover everything from loading hay and corn to hunting and gymkhanas with this most strong, hardy and agile type.

The original Dales Improvement Society was revamped in 1962 and 'Improvement' was removed from the title. Ponies were still registered but there was now an upgrading register too and by the time this was closed in 1971, the quality Dales pony was as we find it now. It may no longer be carrying heavy weights in the Army or pulling a hay cart but the qualities prized then are still valued in driving and riding in all its many forms today.

able to size up which farms had the best ponies too. Several famous Dales breeders were butchers, who got behind the founding of The Dales Improvement Society (DIS) in December 1916. Founding members were also farmers, business owners and Hunt Masters. Following the formation of the DIS, the first full breed show was at Weardale in April 1917. The show was to register the premium breed stallions and there were also twenty-three mares offered for consideration, thought to be the best ever seen.

bred out of Scotland. Their ability in testing terrain and conditions made them ideal for the Dales mines and transport. Used within the mines themselves, they wore leather boots in the water flows to protect their feet and leather blankets to protect against acid water falling from above. They transported the ore to be washed and smelted and then to the Tyne (30 – 40 miles away) and eastern ports for forward passage to other parts of the country. The pack ponies were formed into teams of 10 – 20, 'loose-headed', meaning they picked their own way along the track and supervised by just one man, often riding a mule or ass and accompanied by a dog. They wore muzzles to stop them grazing along the way, which was standard practice for pack horse trains.

# Dales Pony

The Pennine range in the north of England runs approximately north to south, with the Fell pony found to the west of this backbone of the north, whilst the Dales pony comes from the east. The two breeds are very similar and virtually interchangeable until the start of the 1900s.

The areas of Allendale, Teesdale and Weardale, east of the Pennines, were the centre of lead mining in the UK continuously from Roman times until the late 1870s. The antecedents of the Dales pony are complicated, with it often being stated that they actually worked down the lead mines. There were Dales ponies in this area but they were not actually pit ponies. Ponies were used extensively in these mining operations but the animals utilised were Jagger Galloways, a basic type of quality pack pony,

**The Dales Pony Society**
www.dalespony.org

**Height:** preferred range 14hh–14.2hh*.

**Colours:** Jet black, bay, brown, grey, roan.

**Characteristics as described by The Dales Pony Society:** Alert, high-couraged, intelligent and kind. Action is clean, high, straight and true. Knee and hock are lifted, the hind legs flexed well under the body for powerful drive.

**Status:** Priority (fewer than 300). *Rare Breeds Survival Trust.*

*hands high is a unique measurement for horses. One hand is equal to 4 inches (10 cm).

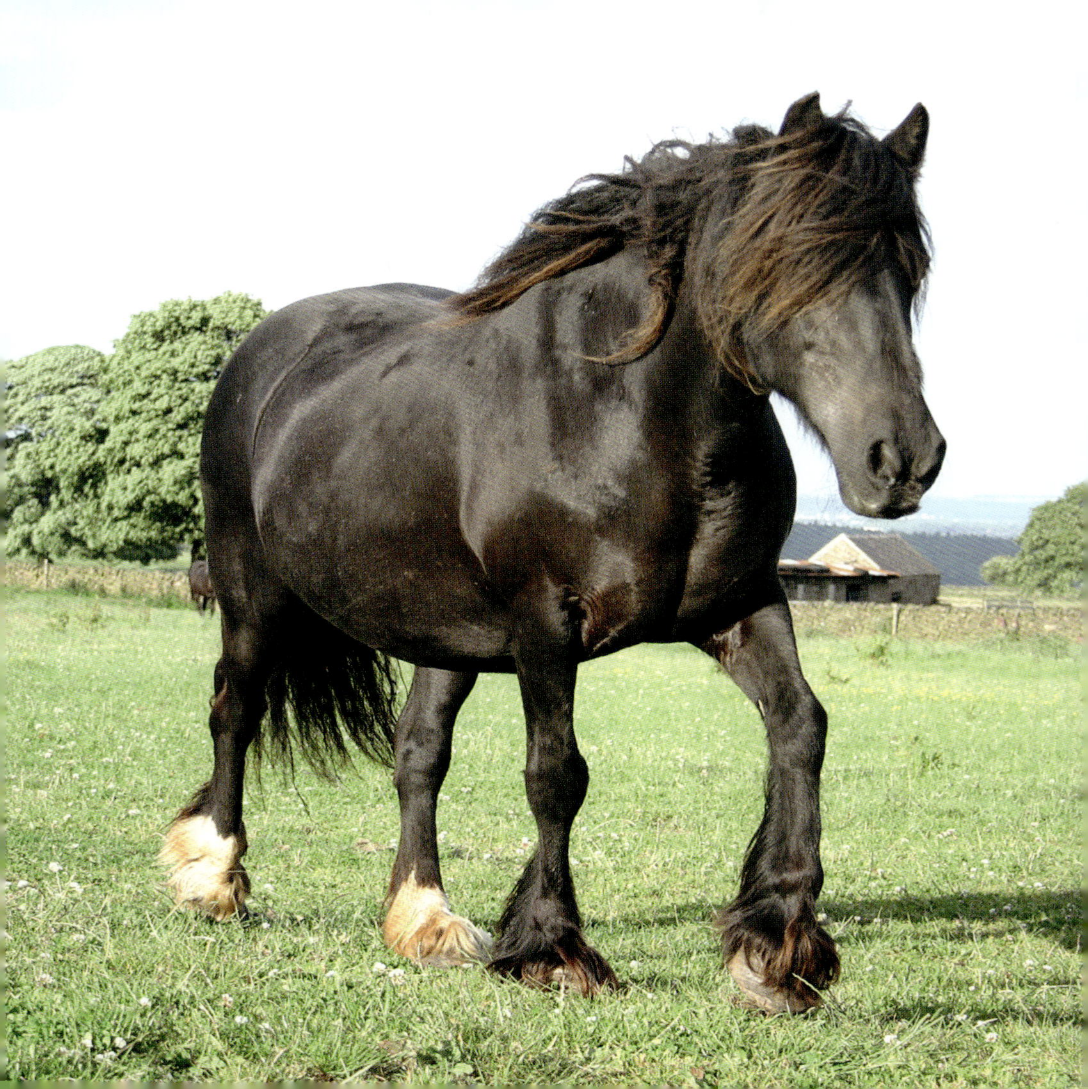

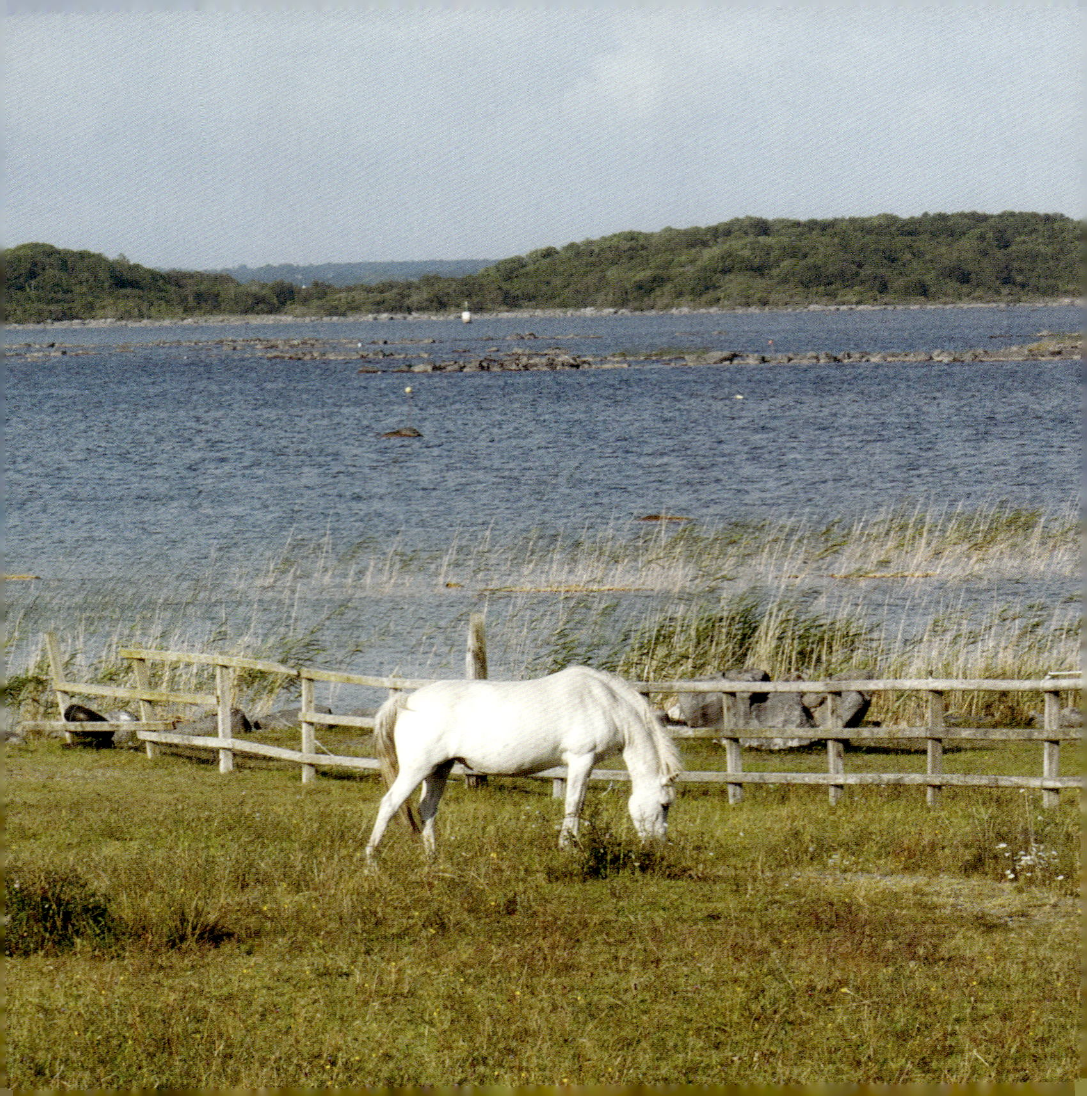

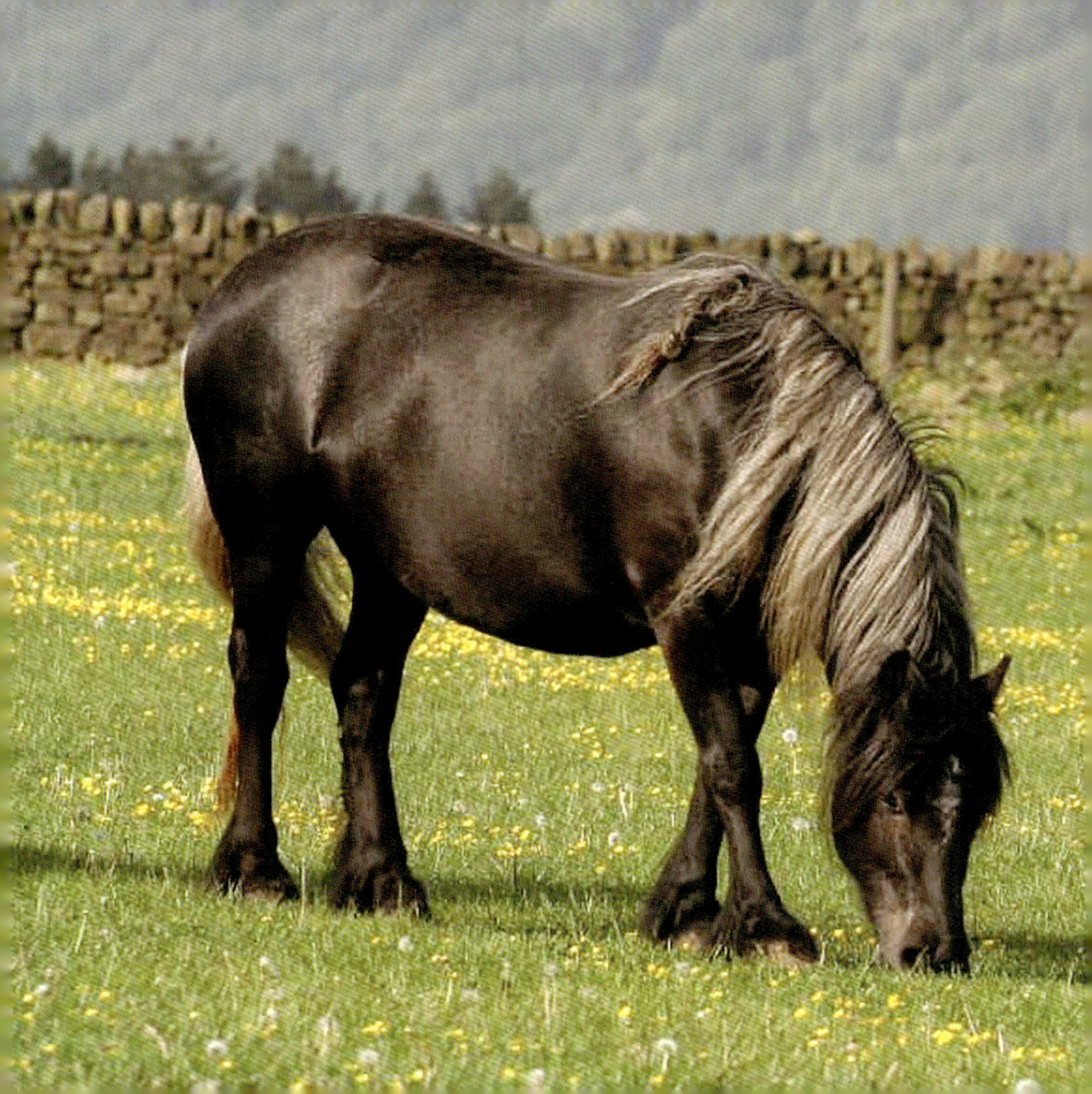

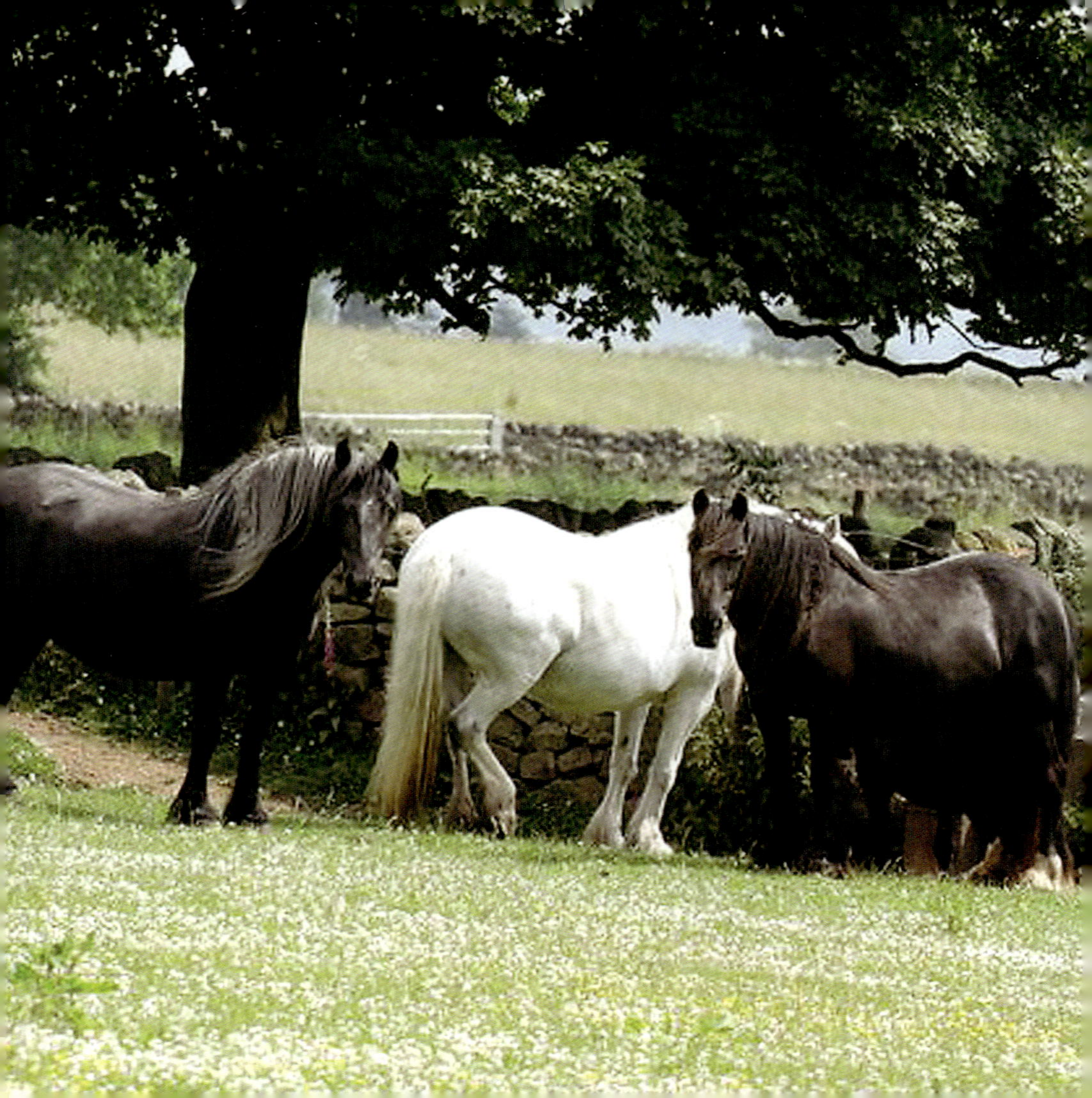

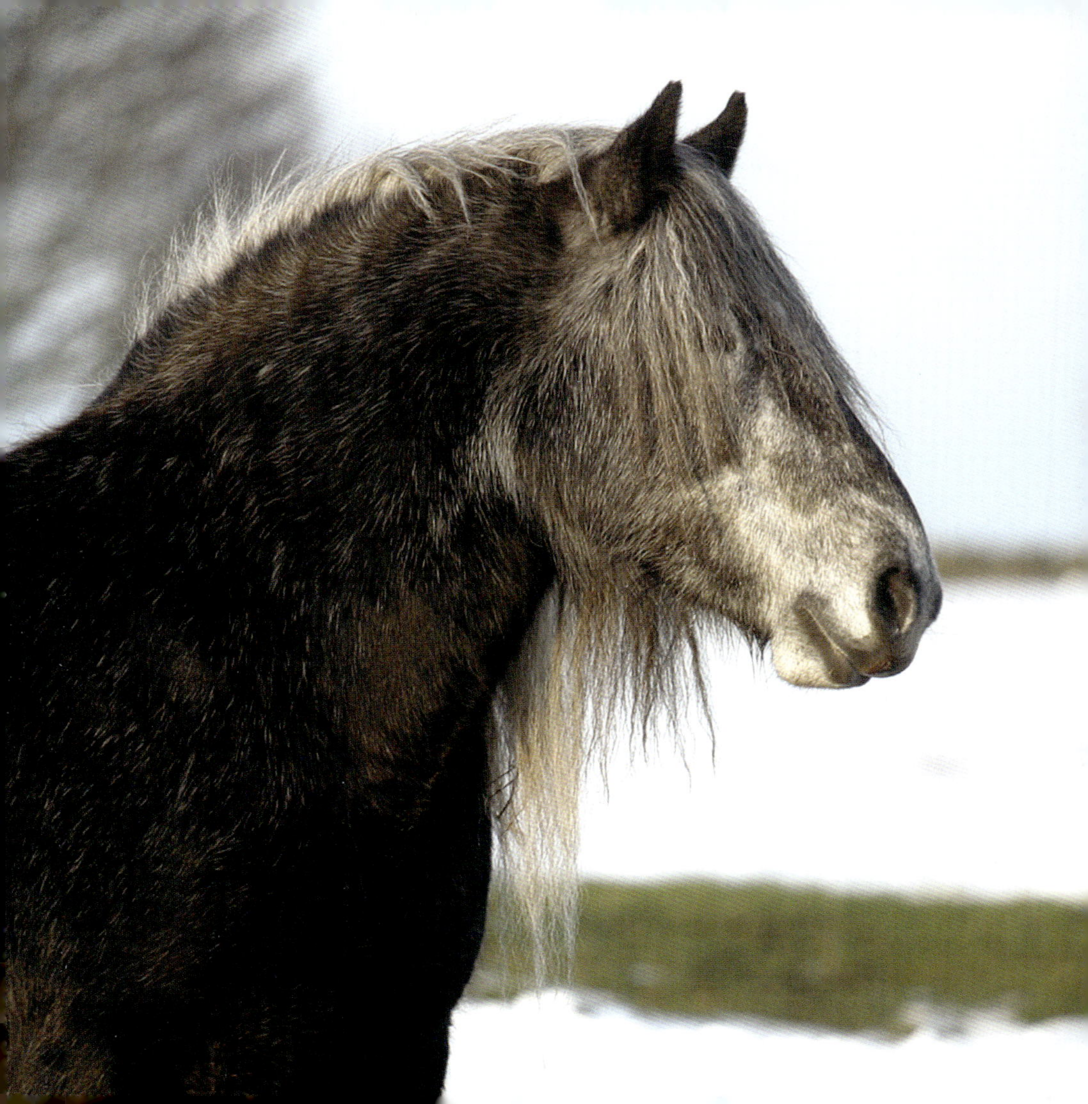

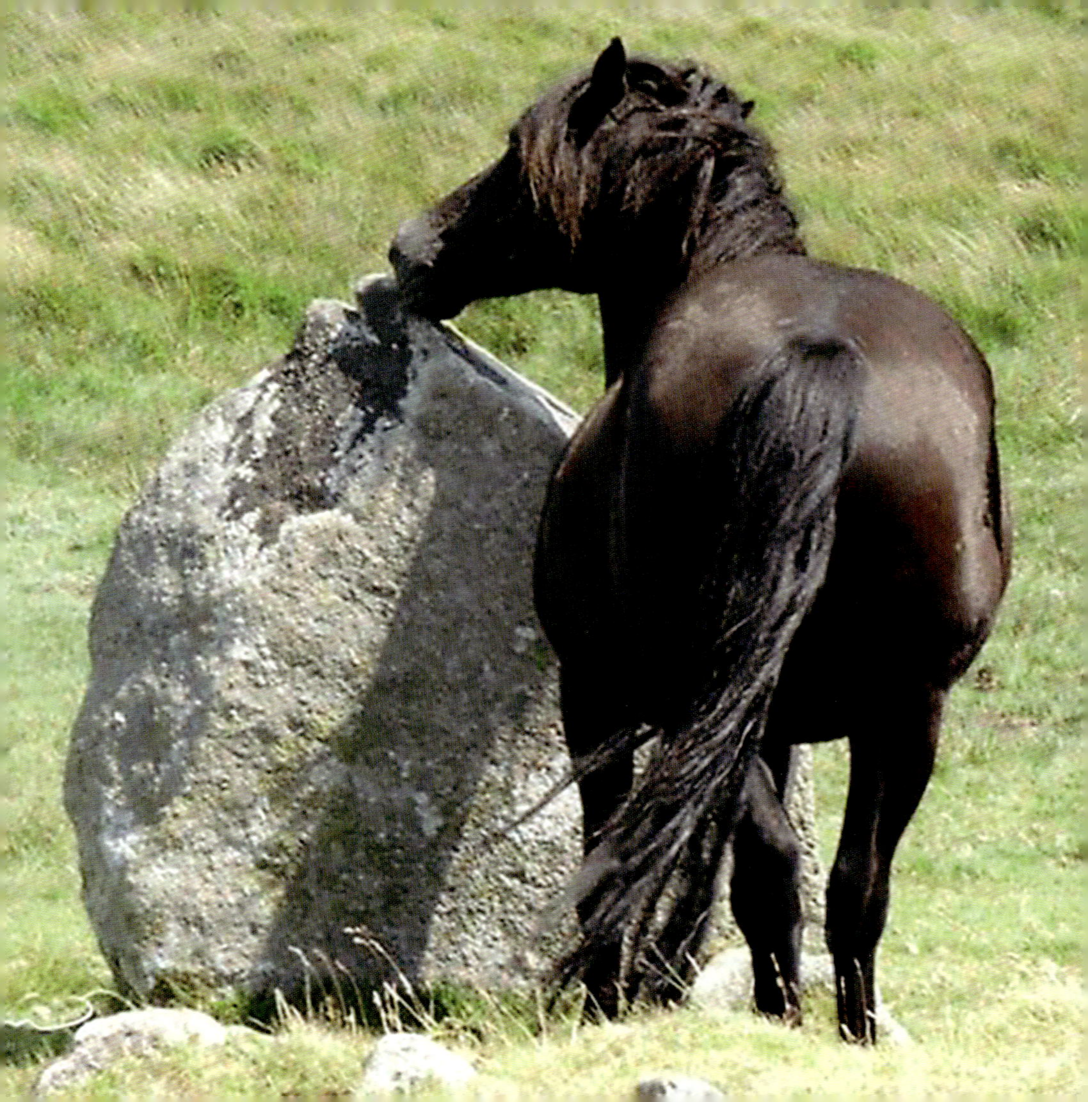

# Dartmoor Pony

The native Dartmoor pony has been living on the moors of Devon since the Middle Ages. Dartmoor sits between the ancient cities of Plymouth and Exeter and it was therefore covered by more passing traffic than its smaller close neighbour Exmoor. From medieval times the ponies were noted for their load carrying stamina, being strong and surefooted and having great hardiness in the rugged and difficult conditions on the moor. Almost everything for life in that most inhospitable of places was transported in panniers by these sturdy little pack ponies.

The first written reference to a Dartmoor pony is in 1012 in the will of Bishop Aelfwold of Crediton, where the 'wild horses of Ashburton' are mentioned. In 1820 William Youatt (a very vocal and famous veterinary

**Dartmoor Pony Society**
www.dartmoorponysociety.com

**Height:** 12.2hh* max.

**Colours:** Bay, brown, black, grey, chestnut, roan.

**Characteristics as described by Dartmoor Pony Society:** The Dartmoor is a very good-looking riding pony, sturdily built yet with quality, like a scaled down middleweight hunter. The mane and tail should be full and flowing. The general impression given by a Dartmoor is of a well made-quality pony with ample bone, which stands over plenty of ground.

**Status:** Priority (fewer than 300). *Rare Breeds Survival Trust.*

*hands high is a unique measurement for horses. One hand is equal to 4 inches (10 cm).

surgeon to the RSPCA) wrote – 'There is on Dartmoor a race of ponies much in request in that vicinity being sure footed and hardy and admirably calculated to scramble over the rough roads and dreary wilds of that mountainous district. The Dartmoor pony is larger than the Exmoor and, if possible, uglier. He exists there almost in a state of nature.'

Until the turn of the 19th century the true Dartmoor was alone on the moors. Then some Shetland stallions were brought in to run on the hills, thus creating a crossbreed of small strong ponies perfect for mine and quarry working throughout the country. Following the increased mechanisation in mining, as we have seen previously with the Dales, ponies not used on the farm were turned away and left to roam free on the moors.

At one time there had been a height restriction of 12hh for a stallion to run on the moors. However, owner/breeders had, by the end of the 1800s, started to try for improvement of the moorland stock. In 1898 The Polo and Riding Pony Society (PRPS) was set up, with local committees to review and describe native breeds nationwide. The proposal was that each breed would have a section in the PRPS stud book. The description of the Dartmoor pony was very similar to today's apart from the height. Five stallions and seventy-two mares were entered in that first stud book, with the size specified at 14hh for stallions, 13.2hh for mares. By the mid-1950s this was down to 13 to 13.2hh for both. The height requirement today is 12.2hh, certainly much closer to the original type of Dartmoor from the past.

1902 saw the Dartmoor committees of the PRPS decree that no more than a quarter 'alien blood' should be allowed in crossbreeding. Eighteen years later, post-First World War, this was overlooked, presumably because so many ponies were lost in the war and Dwarka, an Arab foaled in 1922, sired the famous half-Arab stallion The Leat, who played such an important part in raising the quality of the Dartmoor. (Although only at stud for three years before gelding, he is credited with a quality blood line still to be found in the distant past of some top premium Dartmoor ponies today.)

In 1912 the President of the Board of Agriculture and Fisheries created a committee to look at how to improve the quality of mountain and moorland breeds across the whole country. Mr Edmund Northey,

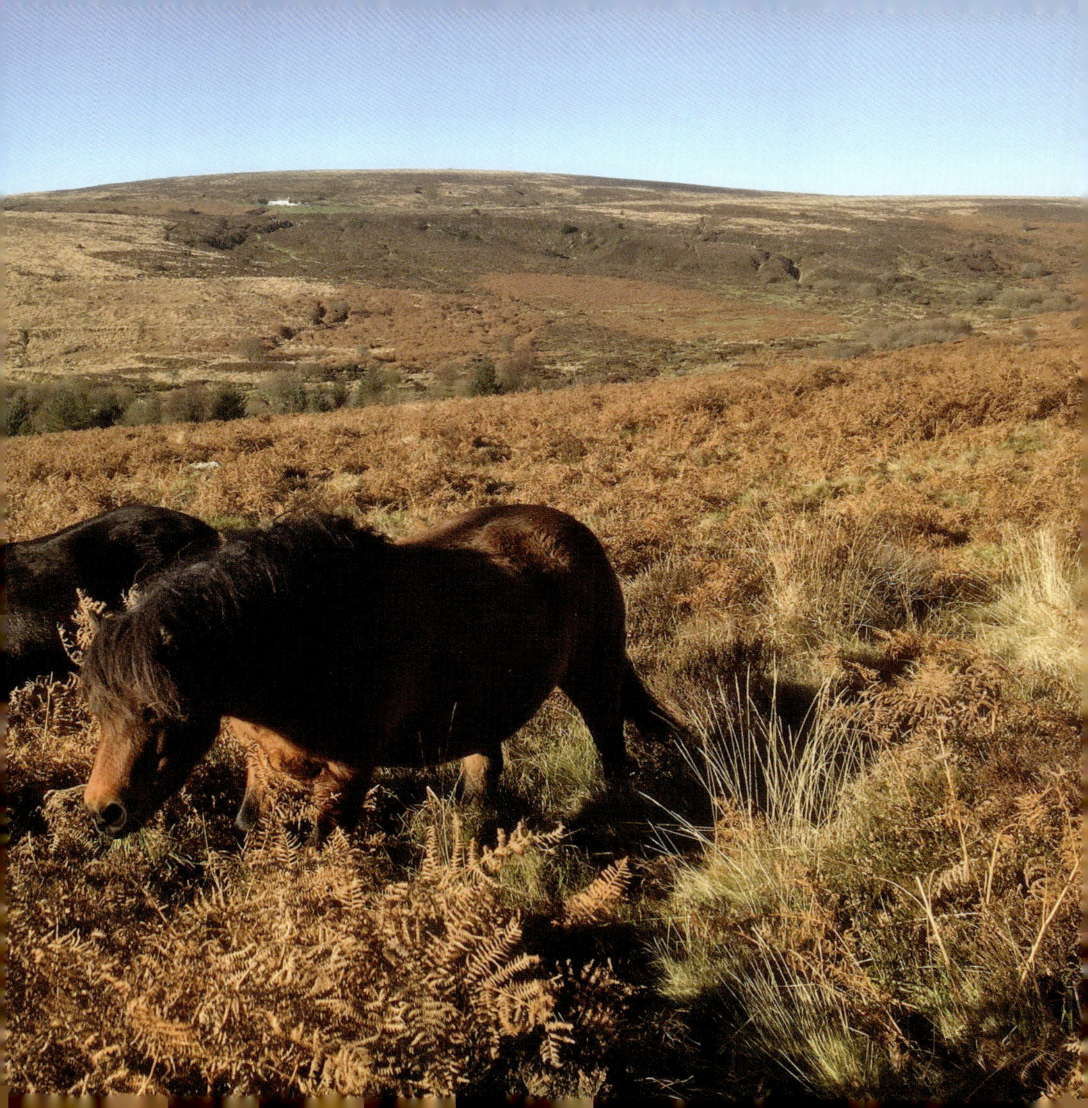

who was a very knowledgeable, hardworking and well-connected gentleman farmer from Oakhampton, offered up several schemes to benefit the Dartmoor pony. The core of his main suggestion was that each section of common on the moor would be divided with a group of villages at its core. A number of stallions would be allocated to run with the mares in that area. The number of stallions depended on the size of the area but roughly thirty-six mares to one stallion. This would require the purchasing of thirty-three stallions. On consideration it was felt by the Board of Agriculture and Fisheries that the Dartmoor breeds needed the most help. Money was therefore allocated for thirty premiums of £7.10s paid annually for stallions of four years and upwards. The stallions were to be selected by district committees. In this way the overall standard of the pony was raised and quality was bred into the animals that ran the moors.

Dartmoor was used for practise manoeuvres during the Second World War by American forces and the ponies suffered. Many died and the stud book from 1940-43 only listed two males and twelve females. It took time to recover but by dint of hard work and the determination of lovers of the breed it did. The Dartmoor Pony Society (DPS) started in 1924 but until 1979 all breed registrations still went into the Dartmoor section of the National Pony Society (DPS) stud book. Since then however, the stud book has been held and is issued annually by the DPS.

Mr. John Coaker, Dartmoor farmer and tenant of the Duchy of Cornwall made a move in the 1980s to improve the breed. The idea coalesced in 1988, with help from the Duchy over use of their land, into the Dartmoor Pony Society Moorland Scheme.

For mares to participate they must be inspected by two DPS judges and be:

i) bred on Dartmoor

ii) owned by DPS members, with a holding number within the National Park

iii) Dartmoor type ponies, not bi-coloured and never registered in the DPS stud book

If selected the mares are designated SR (supplementary register) and come into the 'Newtake' (an enclosed area of land on the Moor) to run with a registered pedigree stallion. The usual maximum is fifteen mares.

Foals are inspected the following year and approved female foals are designated SR1.

Subsequent foals of SR1 mares are designated SR2 and their foals, if approved, become fully registered and are then admitted to the stud book.

The first time the female youngsters are returned to the Newtake, there is a monetary incentive given. Male foals are gelded and move on as children's ponies, a role the Dartmoor fills very well indeed.

All the ponies ranging across Dartmoor today are owned by someone. Those not registered as pure bred or seen as heritage ponies (quality ponies but not registered,

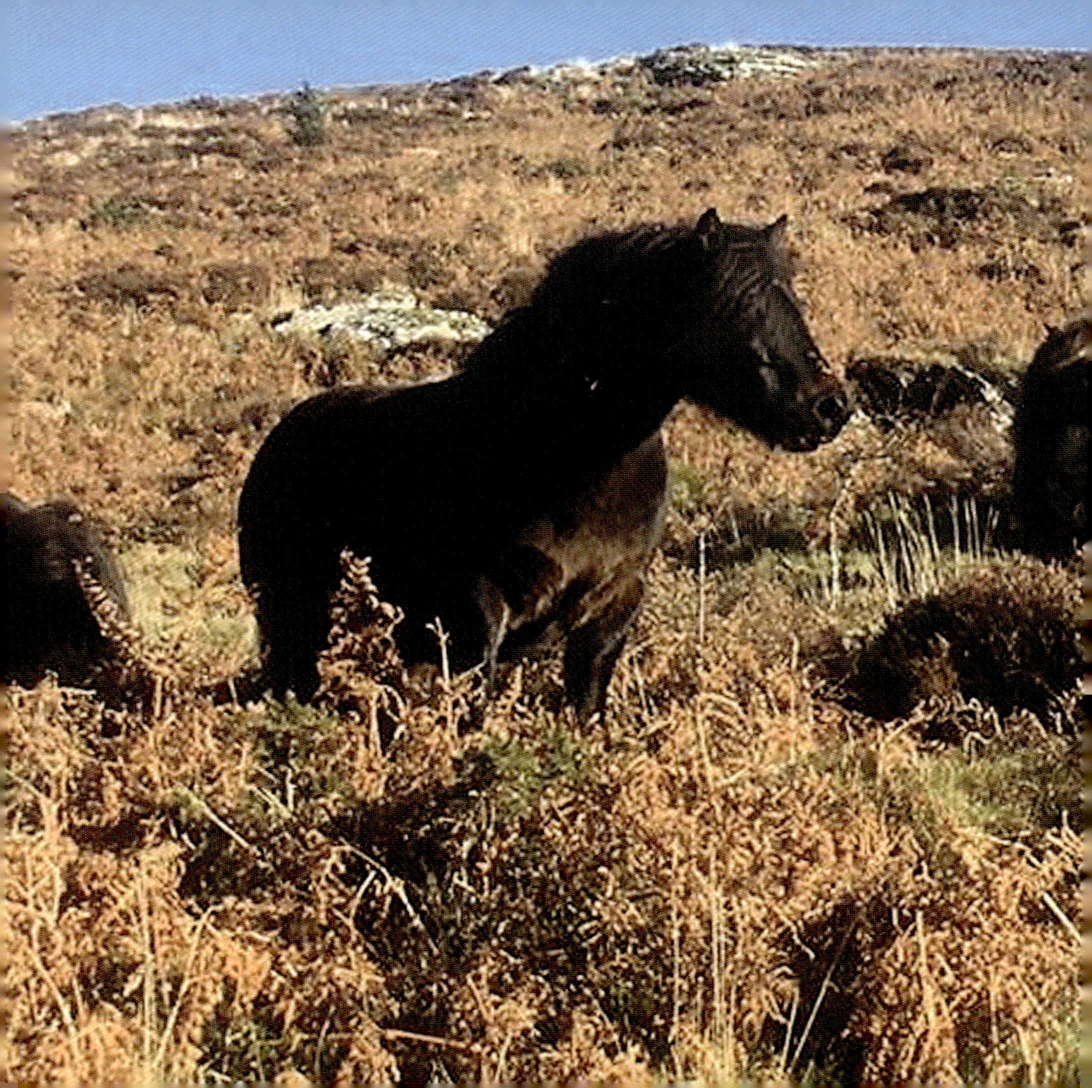

see Dartmoor Pony Heritage Trust at www.dpht.co.uk) are known as Hill Ponies. These small herds come in a variety of colours, types and heights. The Shetland pony type is still very evident on Dartmoor, and Welsh ponies too can be found. The Drift, which happens every autumn, is the point where ponies are herded together at a collection point, sorted by their 'owner marks' and returned to their farms for veterinary checking and decision making about where they should go next.

Conservation, of the moor, the breed and the hill ponies, is a vital issue. There is much discussion amongst herd owners and conservation groups about what is best for the ponies and the landscape. The general consensus seems to be that too many foals are being born. Farmers are starting to run vasectomised stallions with their mares as a guardian to see off 'entire' males who may try to infiltrate the herd. The other side of the coin is to use contraceptives on the mares and this too is being tried. Too many foals every year is not good for anyone, sustainability has to be the watchword as many rescue centres and pony charities supporting abandoned animals will agree. The wonderfully loving nature of the Dartmoor, combined with its strength and agility, has garnered it many fans around the globe. It has found success riding, driving or as a competition pony and long may this continue.

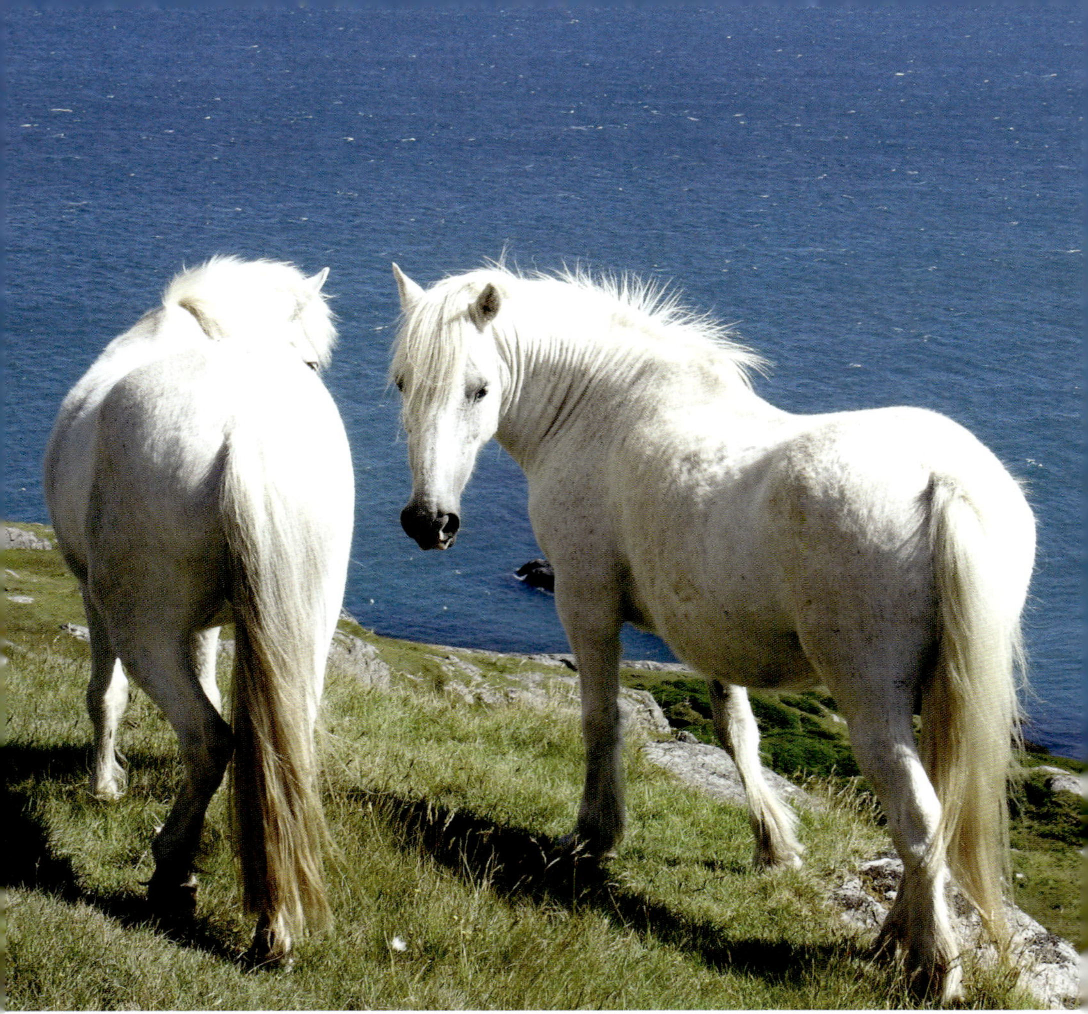

# Eriskay Pony

**Comann Each nan Eilean –The Eriskay Pony Society (CEnE)**
www.eriskaypony.scot

**Height:** 12.0–13.2hh*.

**Colours:** Foals are born black or bay and turn grey as they mature (4–7 years). Dark colours should have pale coloured muzzles and a ring around the eye. There should be no pronounced eel stripe on the back. If their pedigree is confirmed then any colour would be accepted.

**Characteristics as described by Comann Each nan Eilean –The Eriskay Pony Society (CEnE):** Active, honest and workmanlike with good temperament. Sensible and intelligent with a pronounced level of confidence and affinity with humans.

The excellent temperament of Eriskay ponies is one of their most distinctive and valuable features. All Eriskay ponies should be placid and amenable with no signs of viciousness or aggression.

**Confirmation:** A certain amount of flexibility is allowed. Generally, however, ponies must have the conformation of a good horse and, in addition, have those specific points which distinguish Eriskay ponies such as fine legs with only a tuft behind the fetlock... feet, small and neat with hard horn.

**Status:** Priority (fewer than 300). *Rare Breeds Survival Trust.*

*hands high is a unique measurement for horses. One hand is equal to 4 inches (10 cm).

Eriskay is a small island in the Outer Hebrides in the far north west of Scotland between South Uist and Barra. Eriskay ponies are the last example of the native ponies of these Western Islands and their lineage can be traced to the wild ponies that bred in the highlands of Scotland long before their colonization by man. The island has no naturally grown trees but does have the very specific machair grazing found only in north and west Scotland and western Ireland. Created over time by low intensity croft farming, machair is a unique habitat for plants, birds and insects. Its preservation is supported by the grazing of native ponies.

A quote from Father Calum MacLellan (1926-2012) states "Without the people of Eriskay there would be no pony, but without the pony there would have been no people on Eriskay." This encapsulates perfectly the symbiotic relationship between man and pony on the island.

Living as they did on the island in very close proximity to the senior members of the community, along with the wives and children of the mainly absent fishermen, it was crucial that the ponies were of sound and docile temperament. They were used about the crofts for taking home the peat for winter fuel in creels or seaweed from the shores for fertiliser and other light farm duties. Those ponies not happy to join in with closely-knit family life, self-selected themselves out of it and were culled. Life was hard, with a poor diet in a harsh and windy island climate; their naturally waterproof coats and thick manes and tails were adapted to cope.

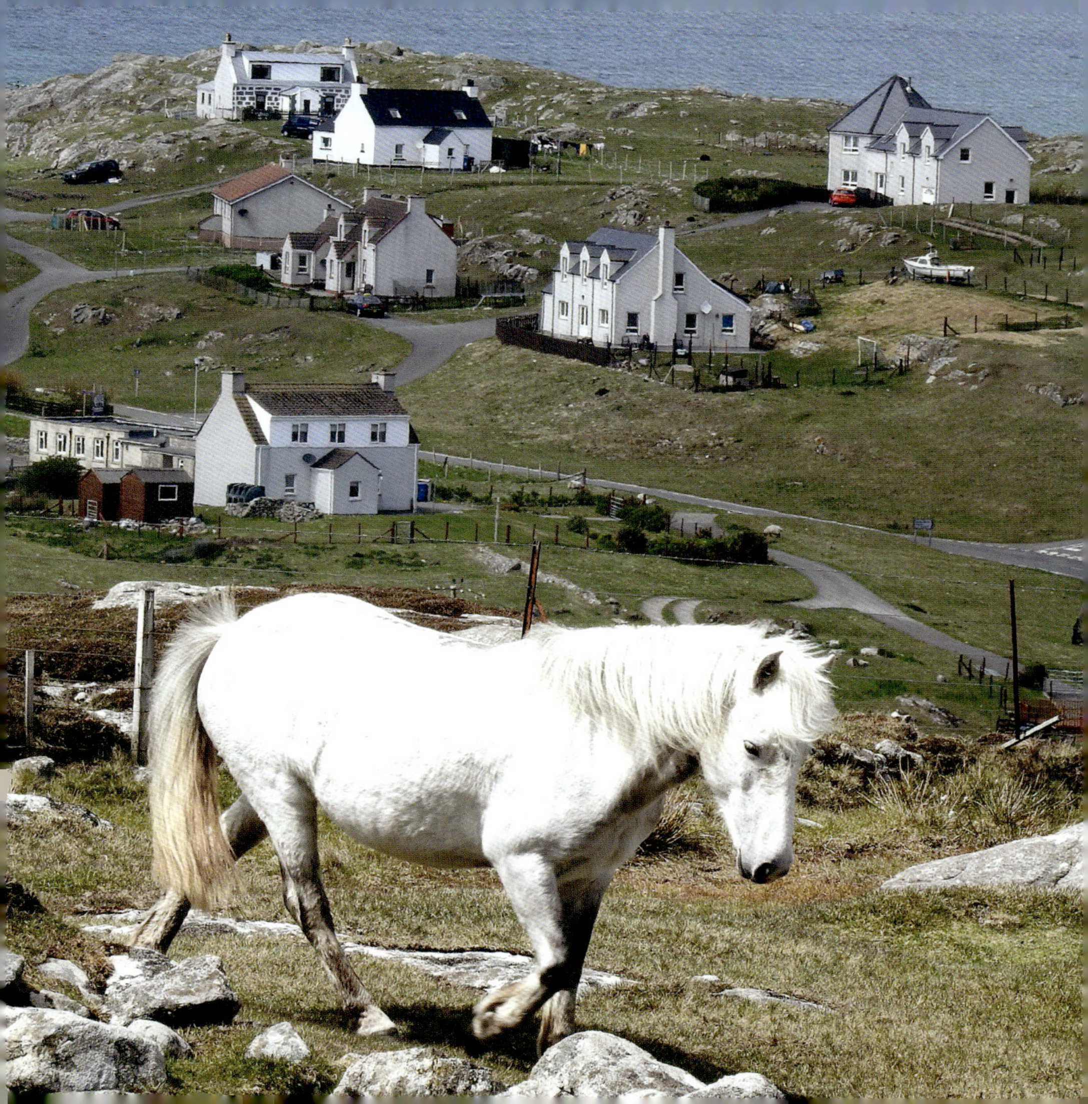

During the 19th century, the other islands of the Hebrides gradually produced a larger equine through crossbreeding. This mixed their Western Isles stock with Arabs and Clydesdales to meet the need for greater farming production. However, as the horse was eventually superseded by the combustion engine, these cross-breeds died out. Eriskay had no pier and the only link to the mainland was a small ferry so, although declining in numbers, the Eriskay pony soldiered on in its pure form until the late 1960s, when there were only about twenty left.

In 1971 Alastair Fraser visited Eriskay as part of his work for the Crofters Commission and was the first person to realise and raise awareness of, a unique horse on the Isle of Eriskay. He contacted Robert Beck, a vet from Tiree and encouraged him to visit the island.

In 1972, a meeting was set up and the original Eriskay pony society was formed, now called Comann Each nan Eilean (CEnE). The founder members were joined by the parish priest of Eriskay, Fr Calum MacNeil, Dr Hill a physician on Barra, along with some of the islanders.

At this point, on Eriskay there were just thirteen females, a few filly foals and no stallion. The first stallion used was another Western Isles type, genetically close to the Eriskay. Prior to the formation of the society, Dr Hill had brought three purebred Eriskay mares and a filly foal from Eriskay to his croft on the Isle of Barra and was breeding with a Highland pony stallion of the Rhum strain.

Interestingly in 1973, a pure Eriskay stallion, Eric, was found on South Uist; the purchaser having presumed Eric to be a gelding. Purebred mares were subsequently covered by Eric on the Isle of Barra. This was necessary because at the time, legislative licencing did not permit the movement of Eric onto Eriskay itself. Three good quality colts resulted, and these formed the breed stock of the island today. Sadly, at the end of the 1970s Eric was put down owing to an incurable illness.

Over the years since, with much hard work on the part of CEnE, numbers for Eriskay ponies have crept up to the high 300s. In line with grazing regulations, there is an annual 'gathering' on 1st May and the gate is opened onto the hill. The dominant mare is led through the gate and the herd follow. The gate is closed and the ponies, often with great enthusiasm, run on the hills for the summer: the gate will then be opened again in October and the ponies will come down when they are ready. This husbanding of the pastures ensures that heavily grazed areas are rested and that the human residents get to raise plants in their gardens in peace. CEnE keeps the stud book of origin for the breed with ONLY purebred stallions being used, and crossbreeding is not allowed in order to maintain the breed characteristics. The Breed Standard set by Robert Beck BVMS, MRCVS for Comann Each nan Eilean 1972 explains why this is so important.

Participants at the annual CEnE AGM.

"Since the Eriskay pony is a native breed, owing more of its characteristics to natural selection than to human influence, it is now the policy of the "Comann Each nan Eilean" (CEnE) Eriskay Pony Mother Society that the natural selection has done its job, therefore we must ensure that we continue to compliment the natural selection and make certain that the breed isn't diluted."

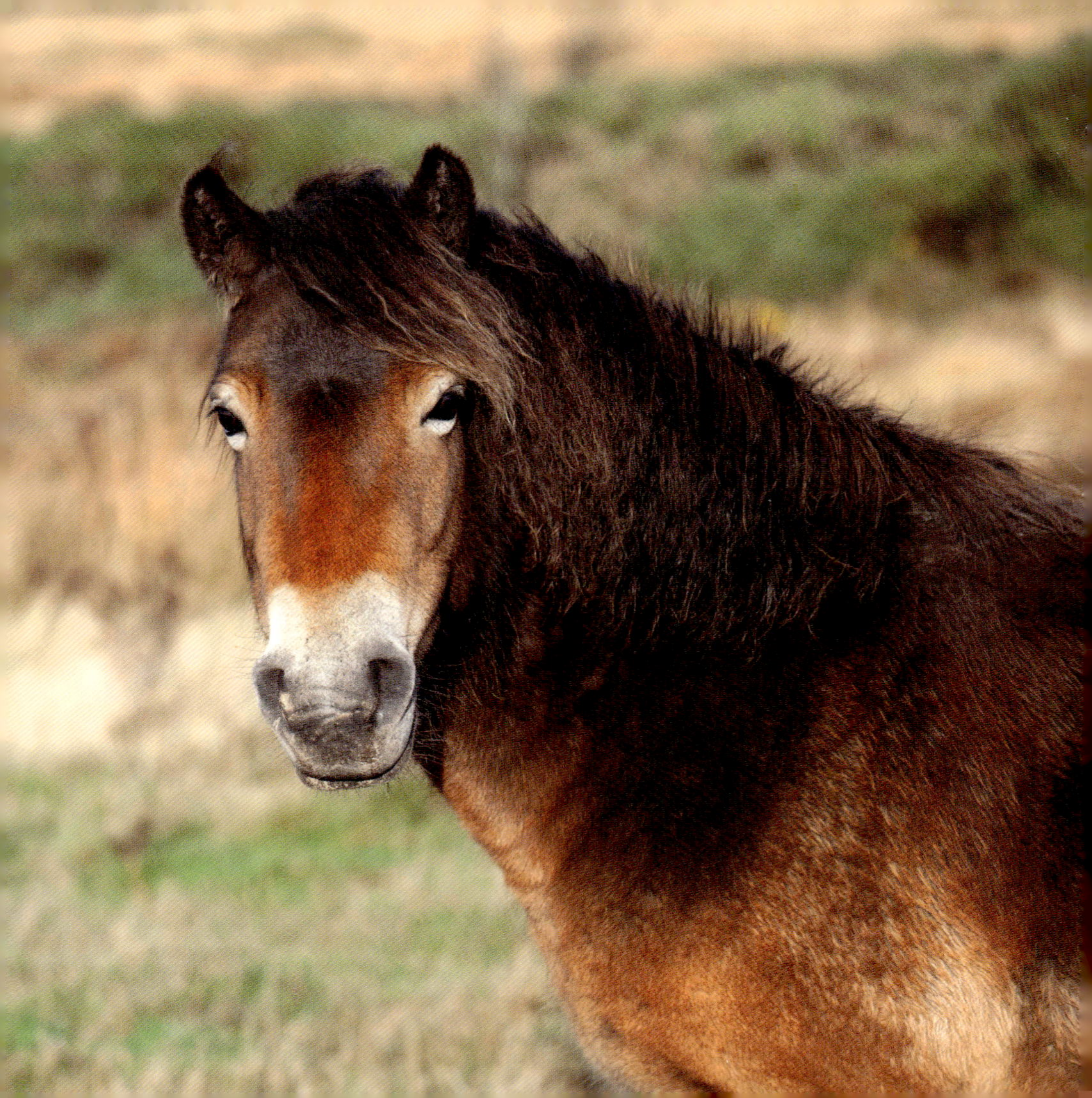

# Exmoor Pony

Exmoor is located in the extreme west of Somerset and the very north west of Devon. The Exmoor pony is very possibly a descendant of the British wild horse dating from 700,000 BC. DNA studies have proved inconclusive in confirming this, but there is pictorial evidence that certainly the Romans knew of a pony looking very like an Exmoor. Did it pull a Celtic chariot? Possibly but there seems to be no doubt it is the oldest of the indigenous species of these islands.

One hundred and seventy-six of the ponies are recorded in the Domesday Book (1086 AD), where they are described as 'equi silvatici' or wild/forest ponies. Norman times saw a considerable number of ponies owned by the crown, with grazing rights given to the Wardens of the forest. Over time the Wardens took

**The Exmoor Pony Society**
www.exmoorponysociety.org.uk

**Height:** Stallions 12.3hh, Mares 12.2hh*.

**Colours:** Bay, brown or dun with mealy muzzle and cream eyeliner.

**Characteristics as described by The Exmoor Pony Society:** Exmoor ponies are versatile, adaptable, very strong for their size. Their sturdy build makes them excellent family ponies being small enough for a child but with enough substance and length of stride to make an excellent mount for a small adult.

**Status:** Priority (fewer than 300). *Rare Breeds Survival Trust.*

*hands high is a unique measurement for horses. One hand is equal to 4 inches (10 cm).

on ownership of the rights, with the job and the ponies being passed from father to son.

In 1818 Exmoor was deforested and partially enclosed, with the last Warden being Sir Richard Acland. He received 3,000 acres as compensation for the discontinuation of the job. He gathered 400 ponies from the deforested land and kept them at his house at Winsford Hill. Some ponies, when the remainder were sold off, were bought by local farmers and so stayed in the area. In the late 1880s Sir Thomas Acland used to have 10 to 15 mares and foals driven on foot to his estate near Exeter. The mares were then sent back to the moor, whilst the youngsters stayed in his park for two winters and one summer. By this method Sir Thomas felt that he was improving the breed without crossbreeding. The Acland family

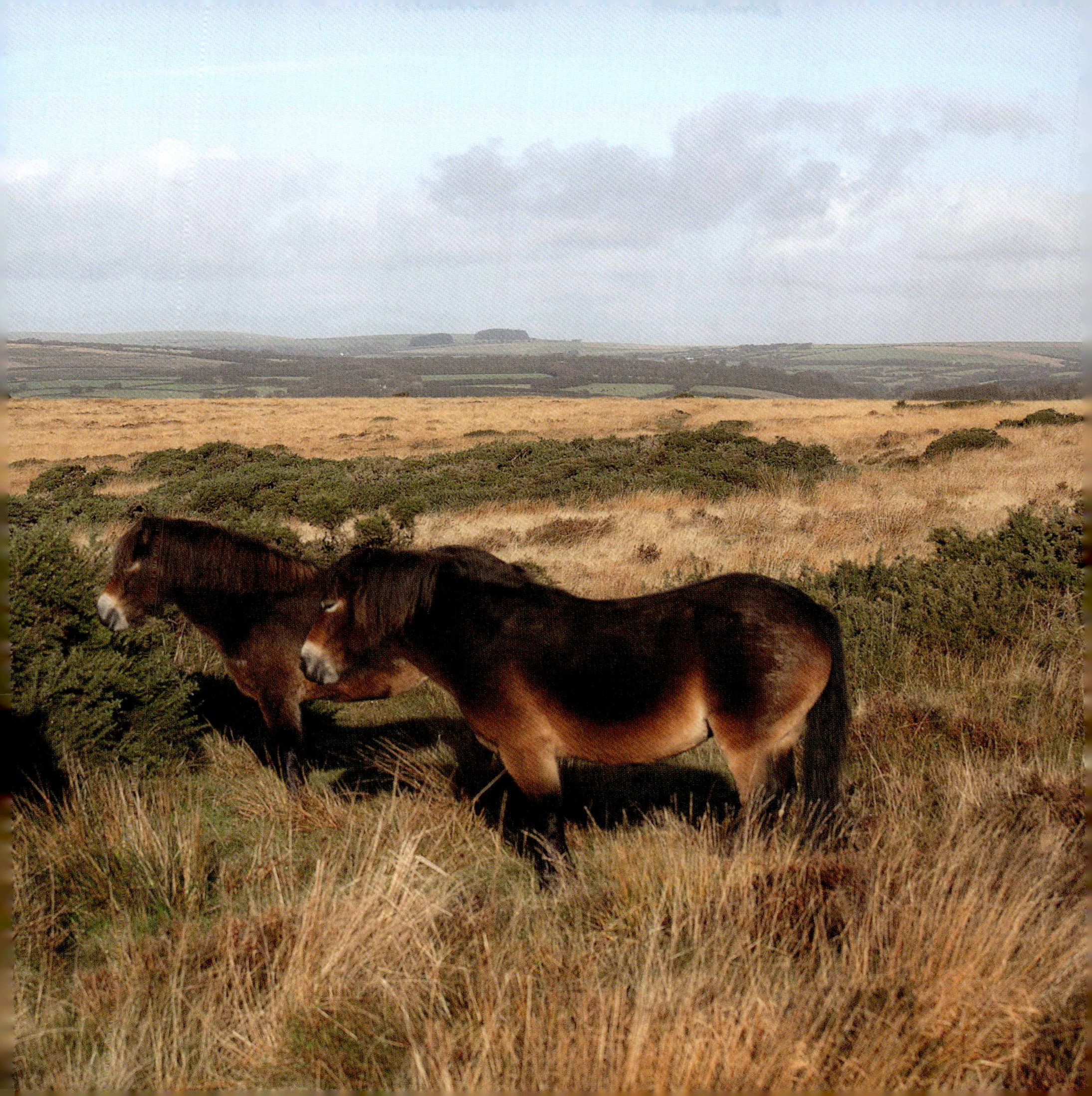

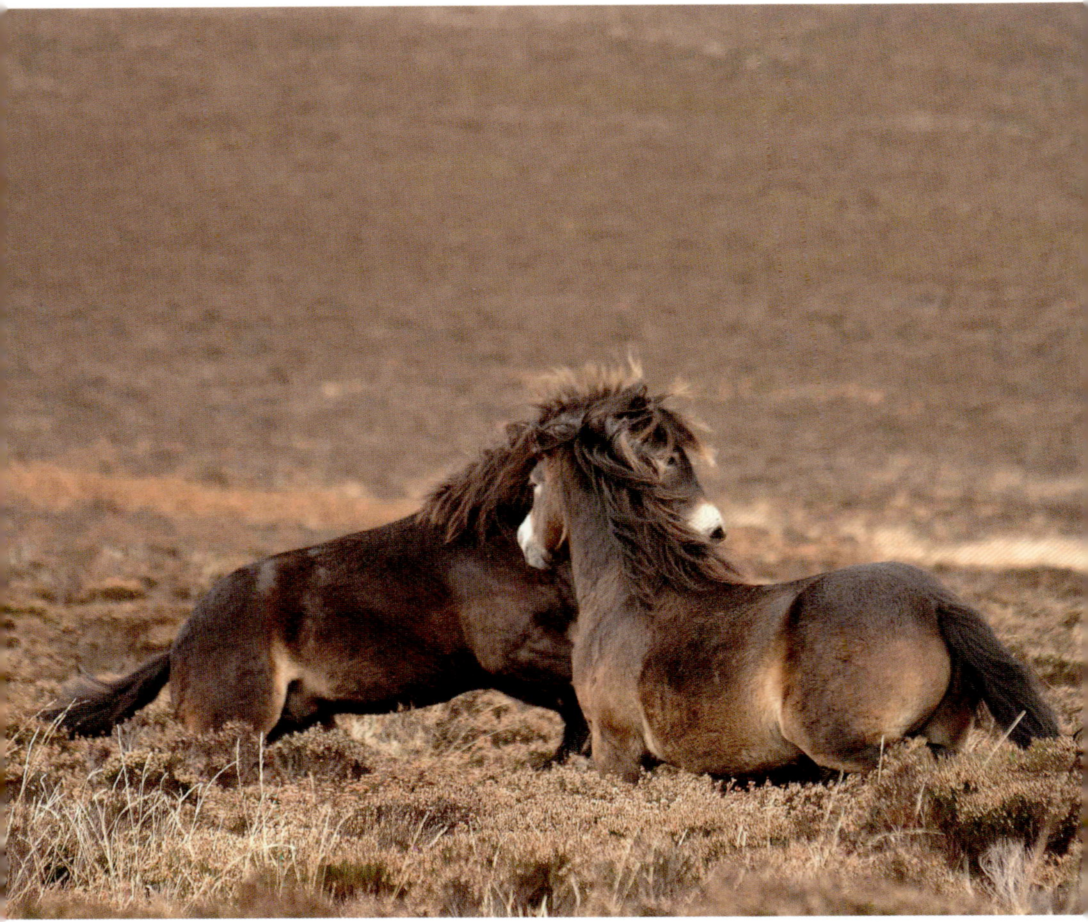

continued to play a leading role in the maintenance of the breed until 1919 when 300 ponies were sold to cover death duties.

There was some crossbreeding over the decades in an attempt to increase the overall height of the ponies. However, these attempts came to nothing as height was bred in but the ability to withstand harsh moorland winters appeared to have been bred out and therefore the crossbreeds did not survive in the wild.

The Exmoor Pony Society was formed in 192´, and stud records (some of the 'by a Welsh pony' type) were kept by the National Pony Society. The Acland herd had been well documented, as you might expect but the stud books were lost in a fire and no full records of breeding kept until the 1963 publication of the Exmoor Pony Society's first stud book.

The breed was very close to extinction after the Second World War Only about 50 ponies were left on the moor, they had been slaughtered for meat and the moor had been used for tank exercises. Today's herds on Exmoor are all descended from these last few and they are now managed on the moor itself by the Exmoor National Park Authority, with some very dedicated breeding support from the Exmoor Pony Society (EPS). Original blood lines need to be maintained and to this end, some breeding takes place away from the moor, with lost lines being reintroduced as they become available. Maintaining the genetic pool is very important so Exmoors are also bred both in the wild and on farms in Europe to ensure that the breed would be secure if an equine disease hit the UK stock.

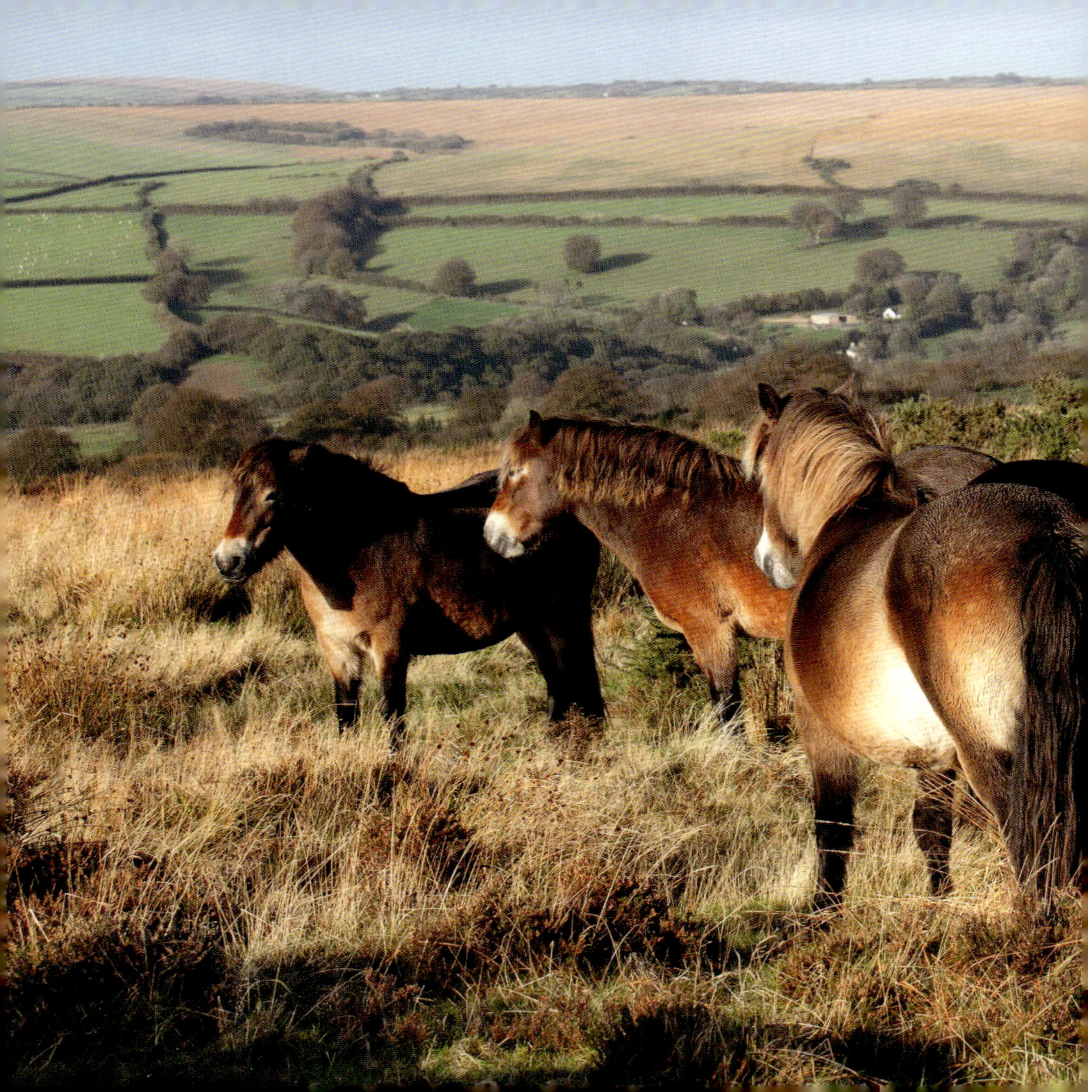

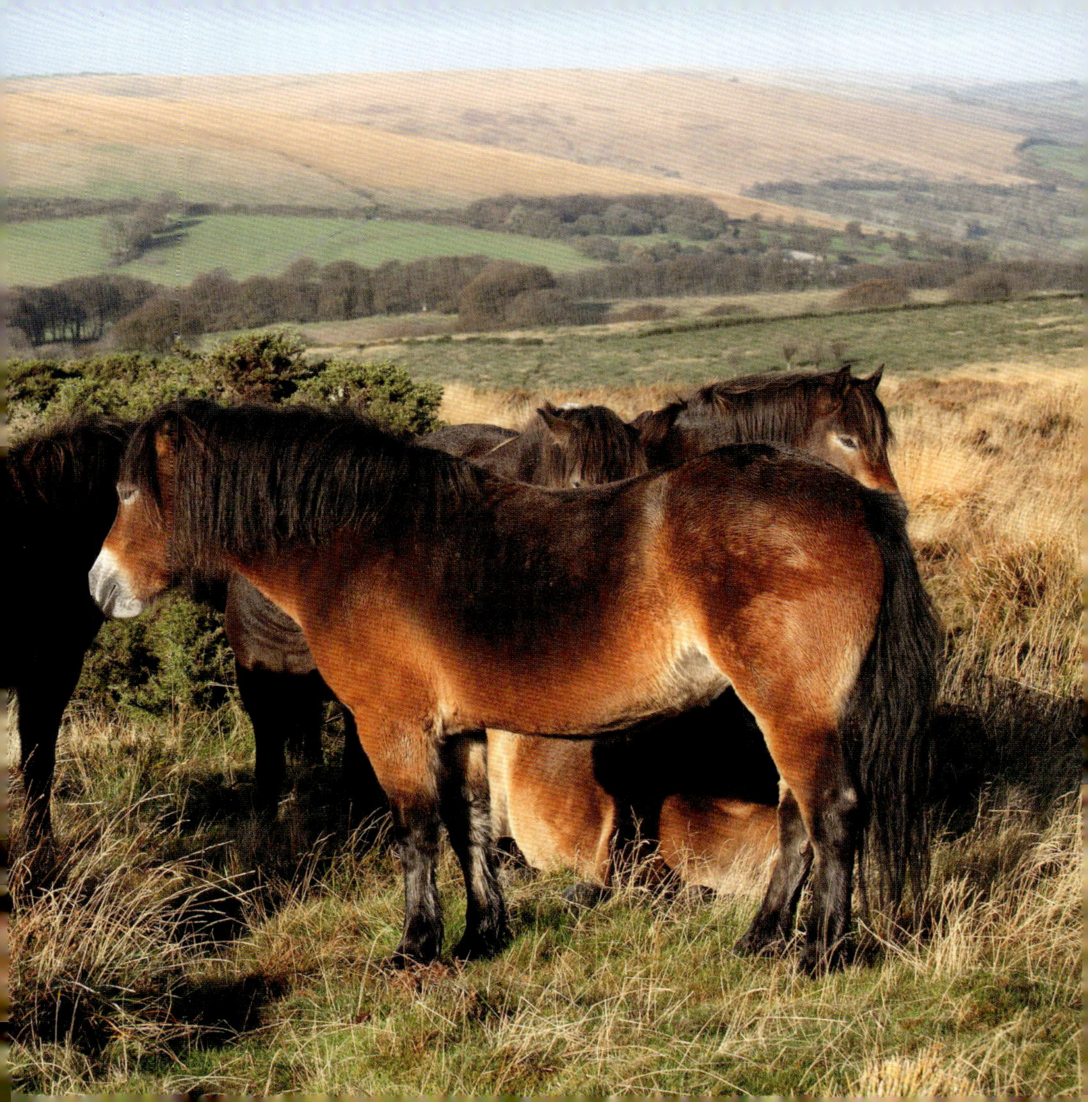

The Exmoor Pony Society works hard to guarantee that Exmoors are the only ponies running on the moor. Fortunately they are easily recognisable so, any odd ponies dropped and left to fend for themselves are quickly spotted and removed. Every foal from registered parents is inspected by highly trained EPS inspectors to ensure that the quality of the breed is maintained. The herds are 'gathered' in the autumn and brought to the owner's home farms for veterinary checks and for the removal of those ponies whose condition will not support them to overwinter. This is also an opportunity to make decisions about which foals to leave to roam and which to find secure homes elsewhere. All foals are microchipped and furthermore, all colts proposed to be used for breeding are EPS and veterinary checked to maintain the breed standard. The work done by the Exmoor Pony Society has led the way in rare breed breeding programmes across the country. The small gene pool for this pony means they are of special interest for genetic studies. In the last twenty years the Rare Breed Survival Trust and the Exmoor Pony Society have reviewed the bloodlines of the stock in great detail. Furthermore, all ponies registered in the EPS studbook can trace their parentage back over generations.

There is better grazing on Exmoor than say, the New Forest but life is still very hard and the Exmoor has developed the stamina and surefootedness of all the Mountain and Moorland breeds. Naturally grass is available for grazing on the moors

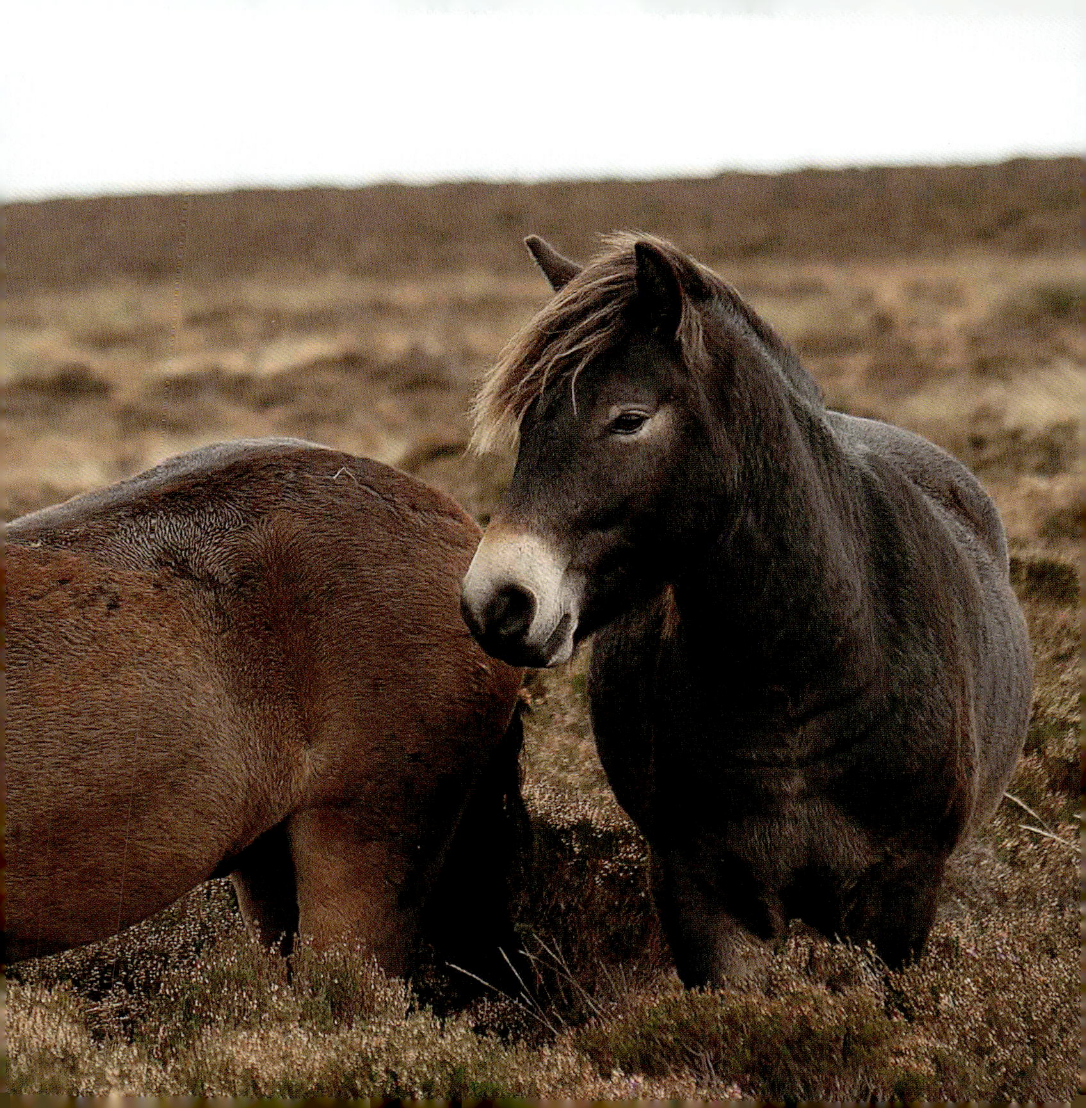

but the Exmoor is also happy eating bracken, which is poisonous to cattle and sheep. In the spring, the new tasty shoots are eaten in quantity, which is good as a medication for any roundworms they may have. This same bracken will be pawed out by the ponies in the autumn for the tasty tubers in the ground. Thistles too are an unlikely favourite, eaten from root to tip, along with the young tips of furze.

Perhaps needless to say Exmoors have particularly strong teeth to cope with sometimes tough foodstuffs. They have also filled a gap in the market as conservation grazers, thriving on herbage spurned by others and thus allowing 'undergrowth' plants to come up. The Moorland Mouse Trust (a sister group of the EPS), the Yorkshire Exmoor Pony Trust and the Sussex Pony Grazing and Conservation

Trust, all have Exmoors keeping their grazing in the best condition. They are also used by county Wildlife Trusts, the National Trust and the RSPB in this role.

These ponies are not fed by anyone, they are left to their own devices, which are well-honed and they live freely in their own time. However, whilst living a free life on the commons of the moor, they are all actually owned by someone. Perhaps not surprisingly, youngsters can be rather wild but if caught up young enough, they can be turned around and make the most wonderful children's ponies. They have the capacity to be both truly wild and tameable, an unusual combination in the British Isles. The coat is unlike any other native breed in that it has a 'springy' double layer with the long top hair laying in such a way as to repel water. This coat becomes smooth, glossy and pelt-like in the summer.

Until the mid-1800s, owing to the lack of useable roads, there were no carts on Exmoor. Everything carried to and across the moor was moved in panniers by pony. Subsequently as roads were built, the milkman and the fishmonger had small traps pulled by Exmoors and produce from the farms was borne to market in wicker baskets.

Today, the Exmoor is seen in driving classes, hunter trials, gymkhana games, Riding for the Disabled and also shown both under saddle and in-hand. However, you must never lose sight of the fact that these wonderfully willing and much loved ponies have the ability to survive in the wild, in a natural, almost feral state if required. They are very special.

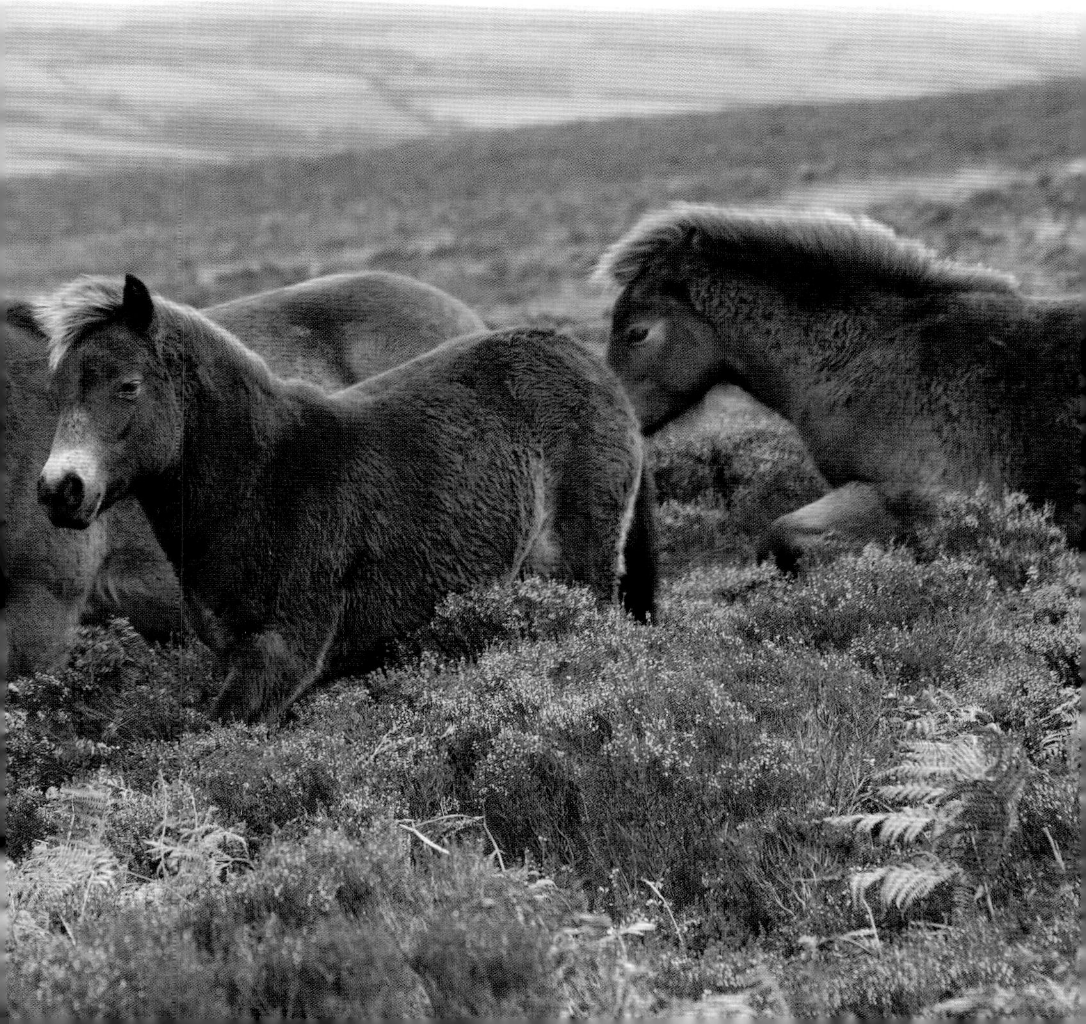

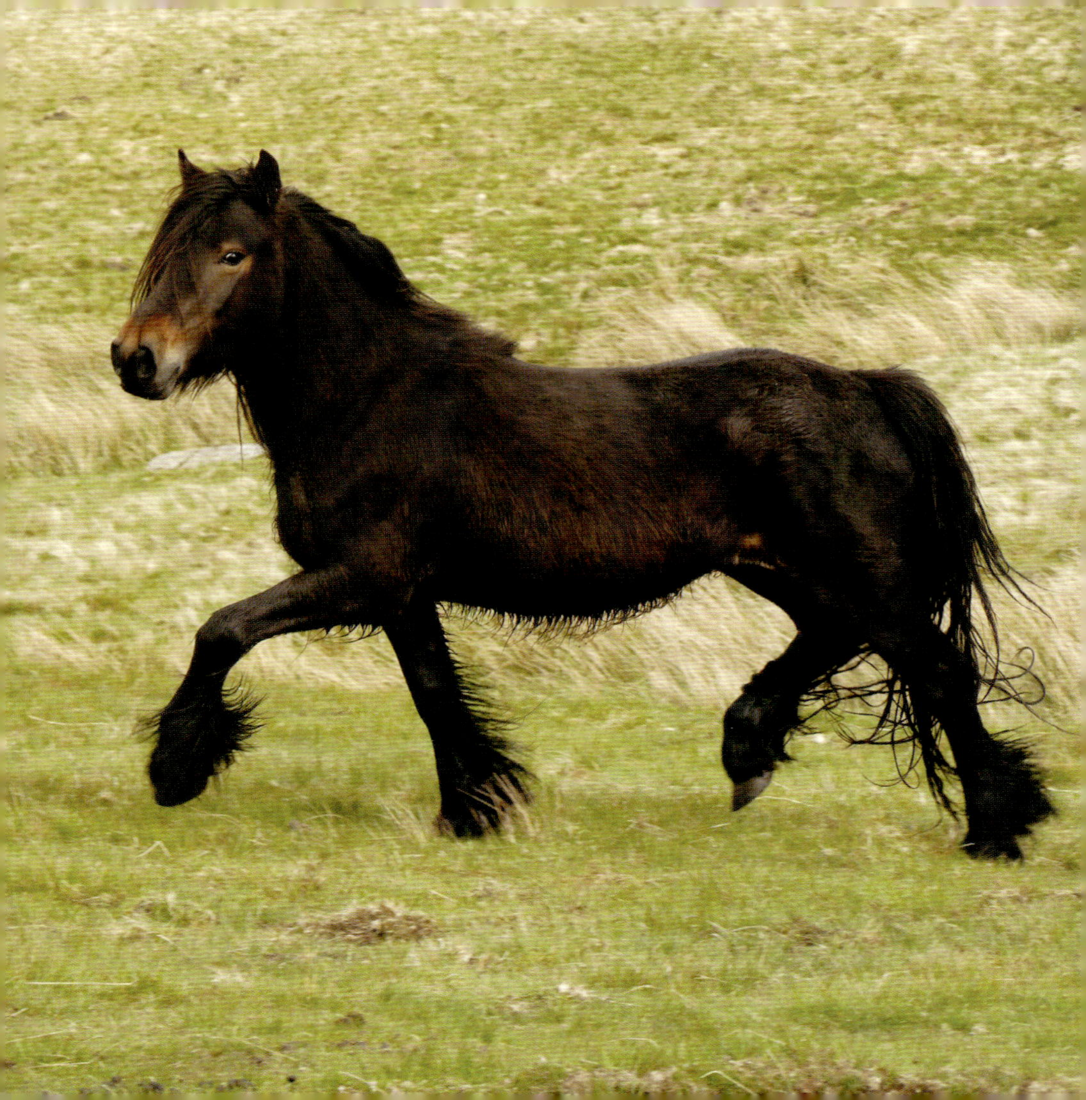

# Fell Pony

The Pennines are often described as the backbone of England but in terms of native ponies, they act as a separator between the Dales pony to the east and the Fell pony to the west.

There are various theories concerning the antecedents of the Fell pony. The primary one states that they were bred on the highlands of Westmorland and Cumberland from descendants of the now extinct Scottish Galloway pony. The Galloway was certainly used in the borders and it would be unlikely that there was no crossover at all. The other suggestion has Fell ponies descended from the Friesian horse out of Holland. These horses were imported with the Roman legions, when they invaded Britain who then brought them up to the north where they helped guard Hadrian's Wall.

**The Fell Pony Society**
www.fellponysociety.org.uk
**Height:** 14hh* maximum.

**Colours:** Black is most common but brown, bay and grey are allowed a star or white above lower eye level, white below nostrils, and any white on the hind leg/hoof is acceptable.

**Characteristics as described by The Fell Pony Society:** The Fell pony should be constitutionally as hard as iron and show good pony characteristics, with the unmistakable appearance of hardiness peculiar to mountain ponies, and at the same time, have a lively and alert appearance and solid, strong bone.

**Status:** At Risk (500 to 900). *Rare Breeds Survival Trust.*

*hands high is a unique measurement for horses. One hand is equal to 4 inches (10 cm).

Friesian horse.

There seems to be good historical evidence for this hypothesis. When the legions returned to the mainland, horses were either sold or left to run free with native animals on the hillside. Although Friesian horses are considerably taller than either Fell or Dale ponies, there would certainly seem to be a familial stamp to their solid yet graceful demeanour. Whichever way they came here, local mares were covered, the Fell pony was the result and many centuries later they are still here.

Originally, the Fell (like the Dale pony) was sometimes known as the Galloway but also locally known

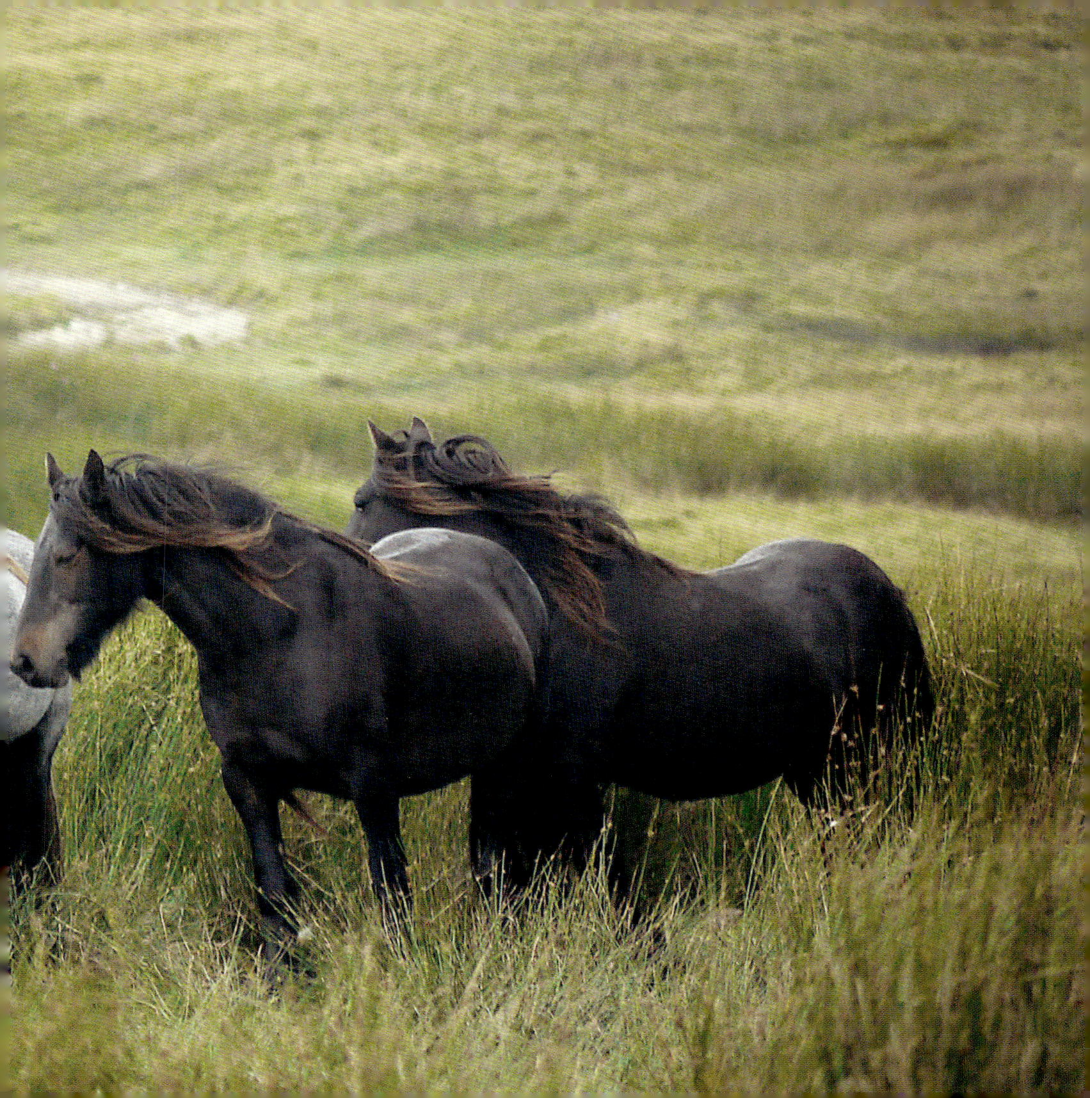

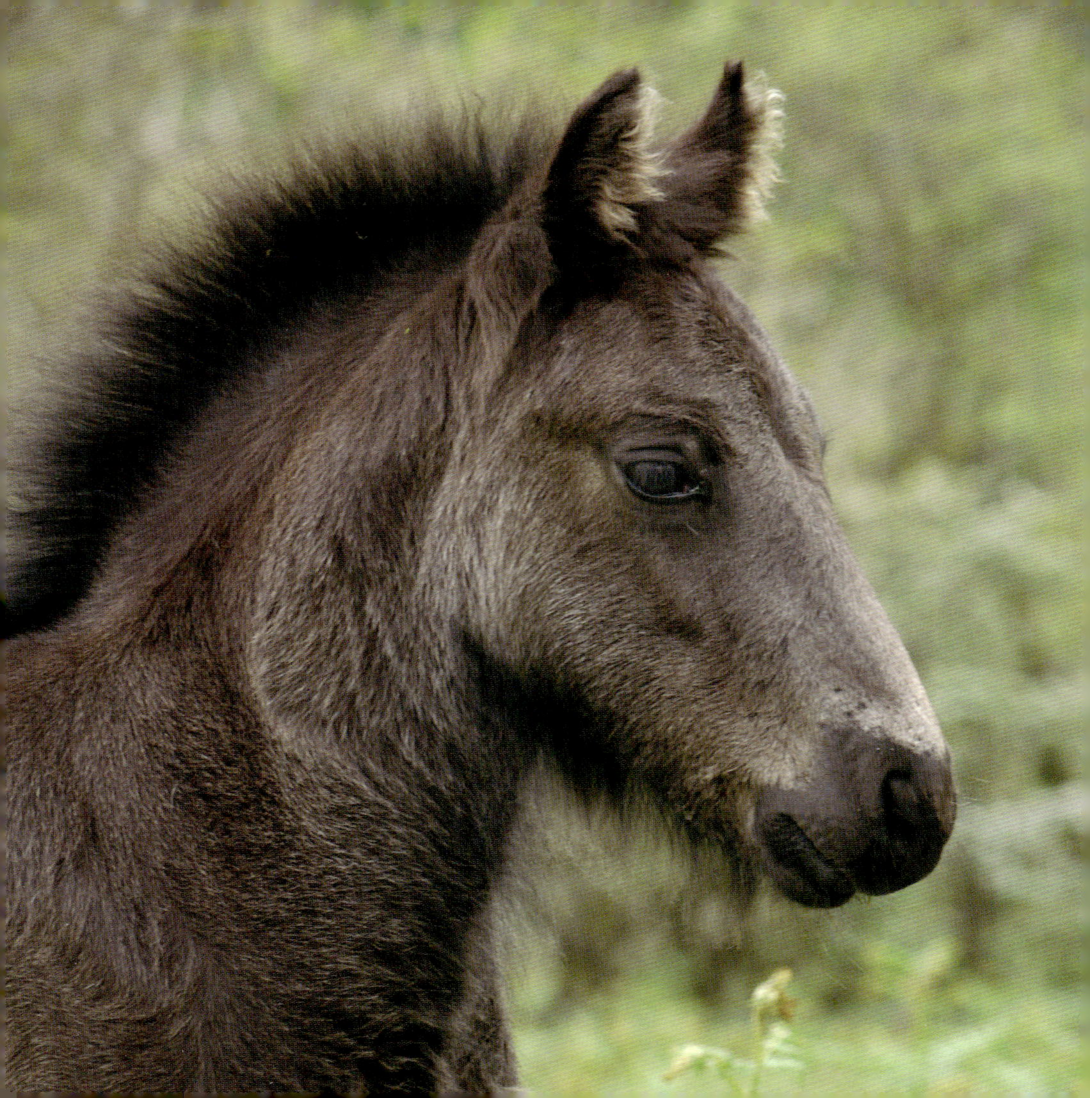

as the Brough Hill pony. This was probably because, at the turn of the 19/20th century, Brough Hill Fair was the sale for hill ponies and the Fell pony was known to be the feature breed of the fair.

The use of the Fell as a pack pony has a long history. Records in Southampton from autumn 1492 show eleven Kendal-men making between them fourteen journeys to the town. These records only show them as collecting items to carry to the north and presupposes that they came down unladen. However, by 1527 it is clear that a proper exchange trade was established, mainly for Kendal cloth. The route took a little over four weeks to travel in each direction. Five to eight horse-loads might be transported in one journey and, by the 1500s, Manchester cottons had been added to the Kendal cloth.

Naturally, the Fell was used for more than merchandise trips to Southampton. Their soundness, sure-footedness, and speed were highly prized. Mines in the fells needed to get their coal to the sea for onward transit and 'pigs' of lead ore needed to be taken to the wash points for cleaning before going to be smelted. Like the Dales pony, the Fell carried large packs of 50kg in panniers on each side to the docks at Tyneside over fifty miles away and were run in teams of up to twenty horses. The drove was run loose-headed with every pony attached to the one in front. The lead animal wore a collar of bells for the others to follow. They would travel as much as 240 miles in a week with only one mounted drover in attendance.

It must have been a hard life for both man and pony, each pig of lead was too heavy for a single man to lift and each pony carried two.

The ponies were also used for other work on farms and smallholdings on the sparsely-populated fells. They were perfect for any situation where a sure-footed and strong mount was needed. Perhaps sheep needed checking on a high, rocky, and mountainous fell or the family had to be carted over steep miles to market, to say nothing of pulling mowing machines or ploughing. In *Westmorland Agriculture* 1800-1900, Frank Garnet describes how *"Most commonly two, tho' sometimes three, and in the western part of the country even four, are yoked together in a plough. They are often turned up the commons during the intervals of labour."*

At the turn of the 19th century, when Fell and Dales ponies were still conjoined in people's minds, Fell pony numbers started to decline. Small herds of up to twenty ran on the hills, they were not fed by anyone and, after an extremely hard winter, would come up to spring in very poor condition. As had happened with other native breeds, a committee to assess the 'characteristics of the breed was gathered. 1898 saw the formation of the Fell Pony Committee and a section was opened in 1899 for the Fell pony in the Polo and Riding Pony Stud Book. Subsequently, the Fell Pony Society began in 1919 and the Society as it is today was formed in 1922.

Unlike the Dales Pony Committee, who were happy to cross with other breeds to 'improve' the Dales, the Fell pony group decided they would try to keep the stock as pure as

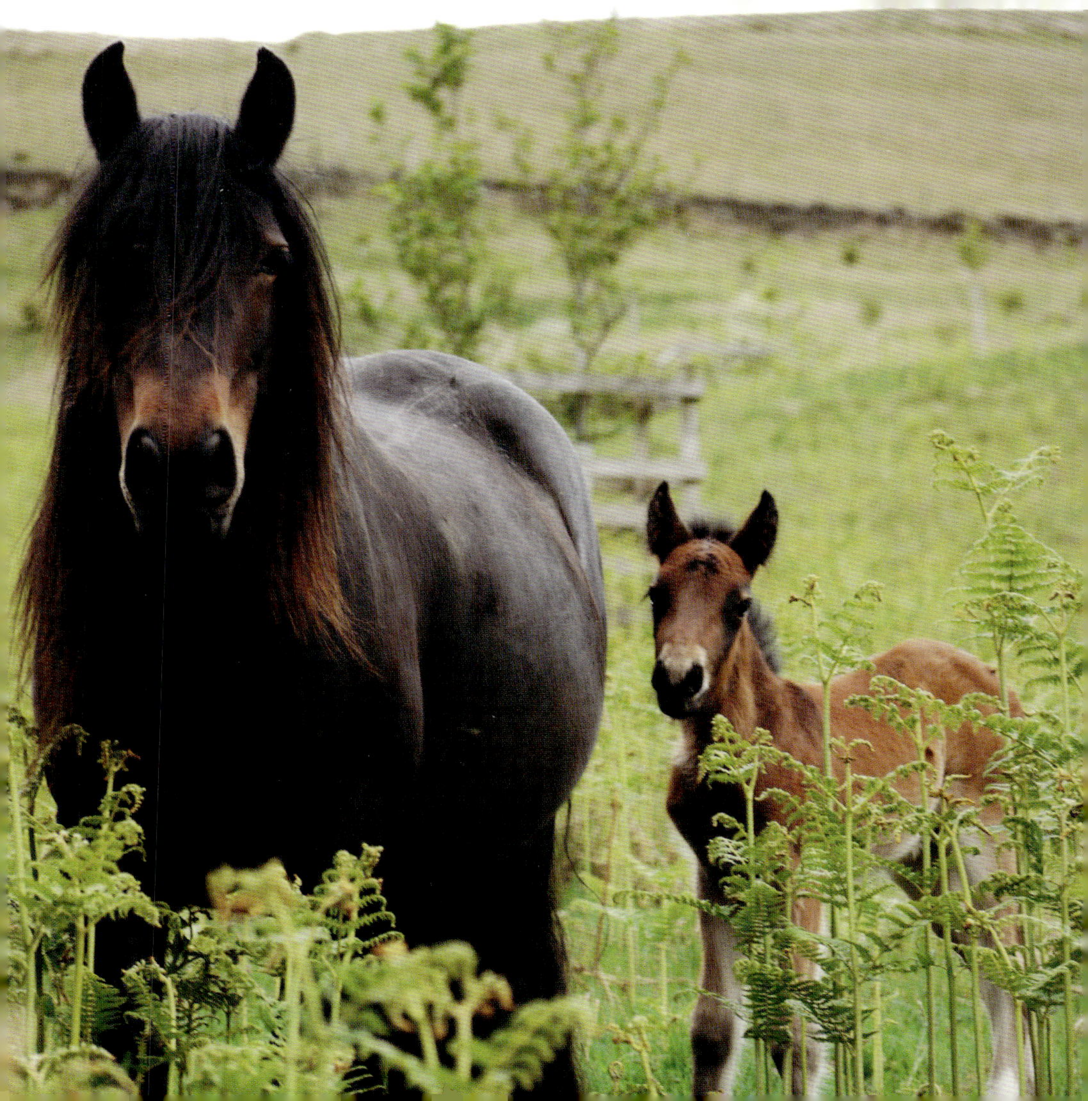

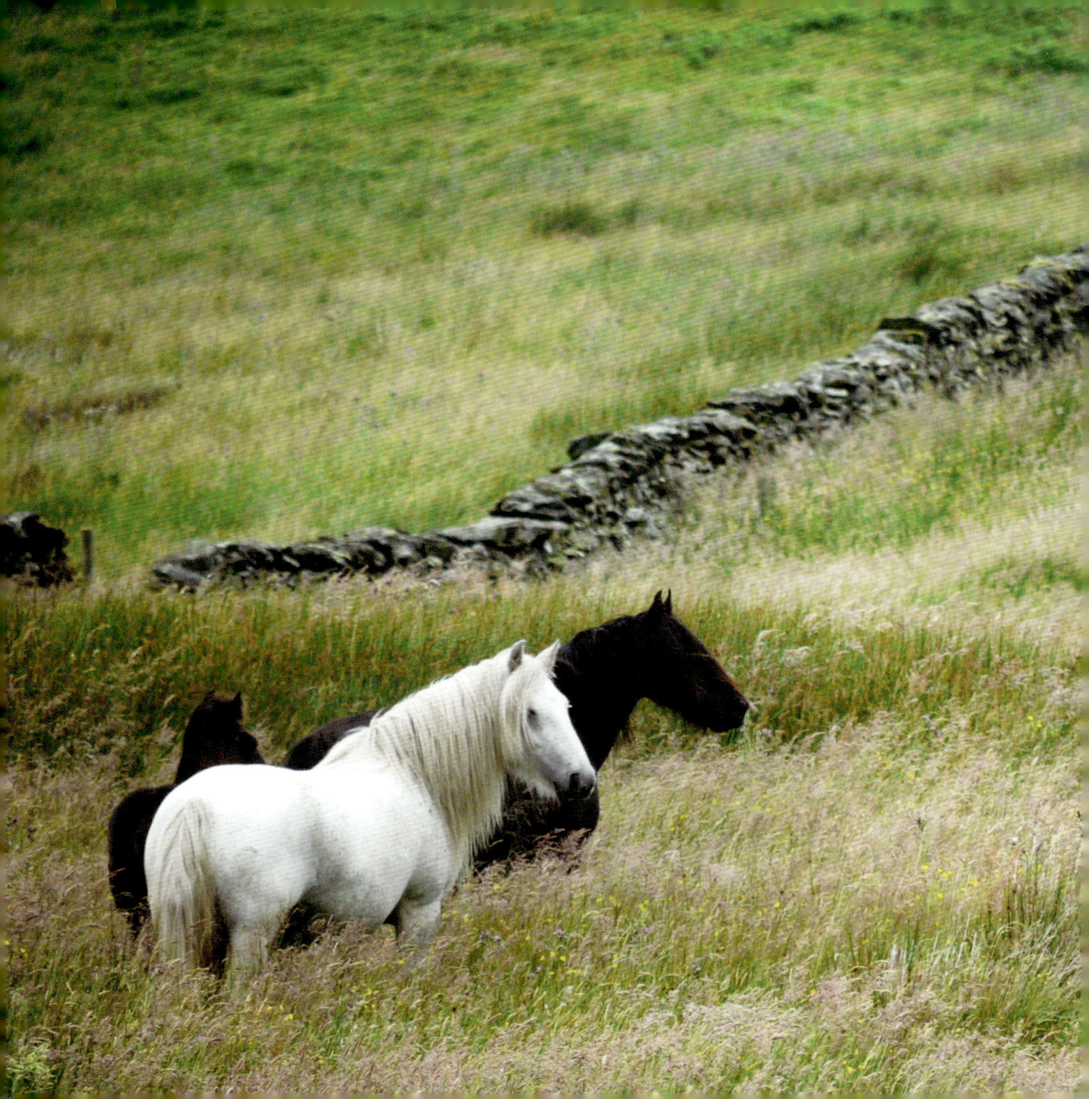

possible. The Fell pony is known for breeding most true to type of all the native ponies. Starting in 1911 the Board of Agriculture gave a £30 prize for the best stallion at four towns in the fells. These animals would be accepted for registration in the stud book. Their owners would then offer them on a 'circuit' to cover mares in Hesket, Newmarket, Keswick, Shap, Appleby, Kirkby Stephen and Middleton. The service fee was not to be greater than 10/-. For example, in 1923 one stallion, Mountain Ranger, travelled nearly 90 miles in one week, with his owner Joe Baxter walking beside him. Stud cards were produced to advertise the stallions on the round. Perhaps these were, for local village boys, the forerunner of the later cigarette cards. We know about these stud cards because they were collected.

There are several strains of ponies from certain stallions and mares that can still be seen in the breeding of the animals of today. One of the names that stands out is Lingcropper, which interestingly appears in both Fell and Dales strains. He was found grazing the 'ling' or heather on Stainmore in Westmorland, tacked up but without a rider, who was presumed to have been killed in a border raid. He subsequently ran the mail from Penrith to Keswick for twelve years unbroken, a distance of approximately eighteen miles. His four generations later progeny Lingcropper Again, foaled in 1900, has a note beside his stud book entry: "Between the years 1880 and 1902...the ancestors of this stallion won for his breeder more than a hundred first and second prizes."

The Lake District country sport of trotting was always popular and reported in detail in local newspapers. Fell ponies gained a reputation for their trotting abilities and one, Little Jean, famously covered a mile in three minutes carrying a 10 stone man. Little Jean was only 12.1hh! By its very nature, the trotting community selected those animals that would shine, and that strength and quality in the trot can still be seen in the breed today. It cannot be overemphasised how important trotting was in the days before television. A race meeting was a grand day out for all the family and was often attached to a horse show or fair.

In recent times the Fell pony has proved its worth as the ultimate all-round family pony. Strong enough to carry an adult and fast enough to give a keen pony-clubber a good time too. Their natural sure-footedness makes them ideal for trekking and working with the disabled and they have cut a groove in the world of driving as well. The ultimate 'ride & drive' pony.

Their pack-pony abilities are still being used to carry supplies and tools to inaccessible hill and mountain places needing repairs, and their ability to survive on slim pickings make them useful conservation grazers. There are no open wild fells as there were in the past. Fell ponies are still run semi-wild on acres of common land attached to farms with fell rights. This quality native pony still endures.

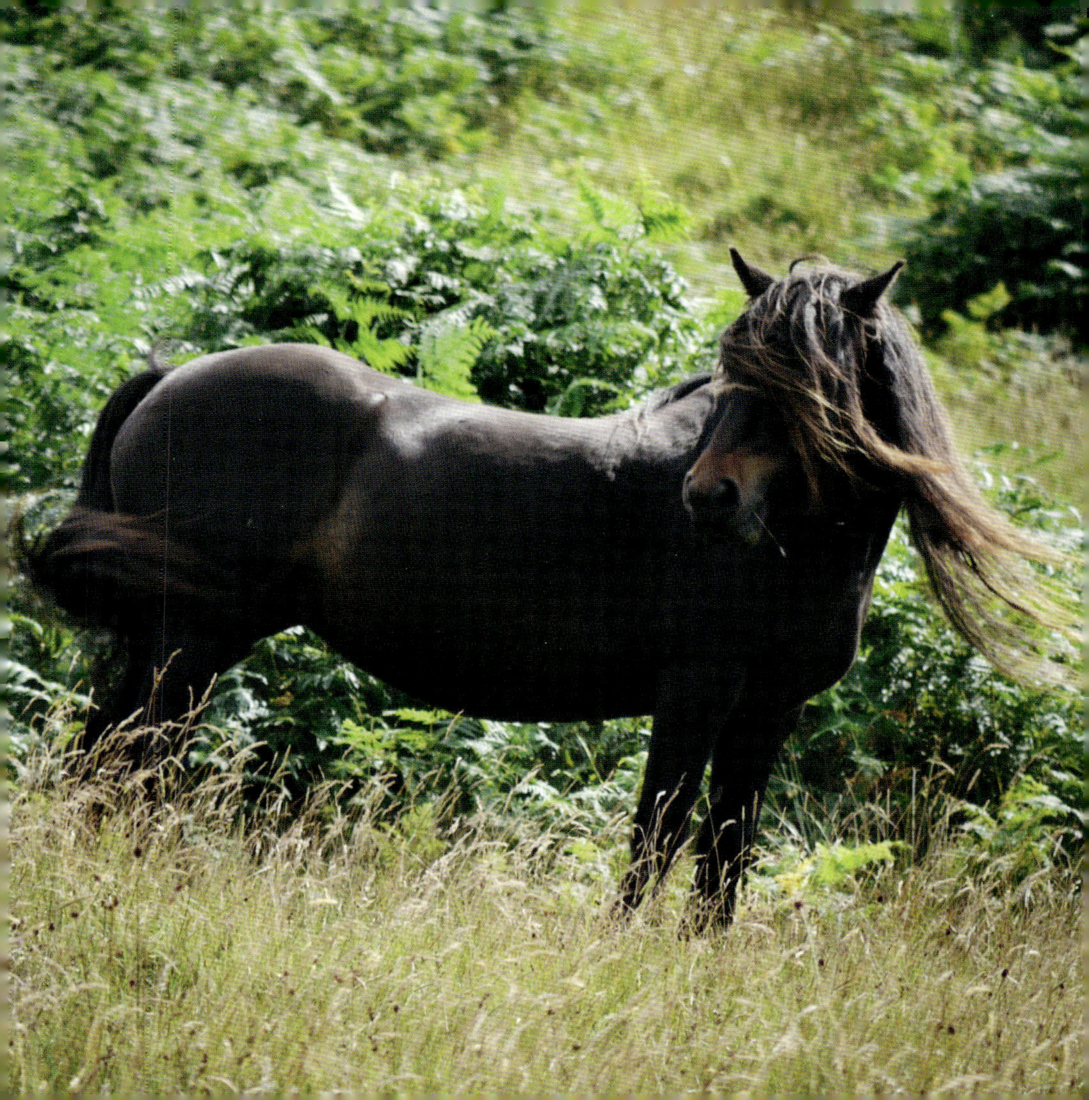

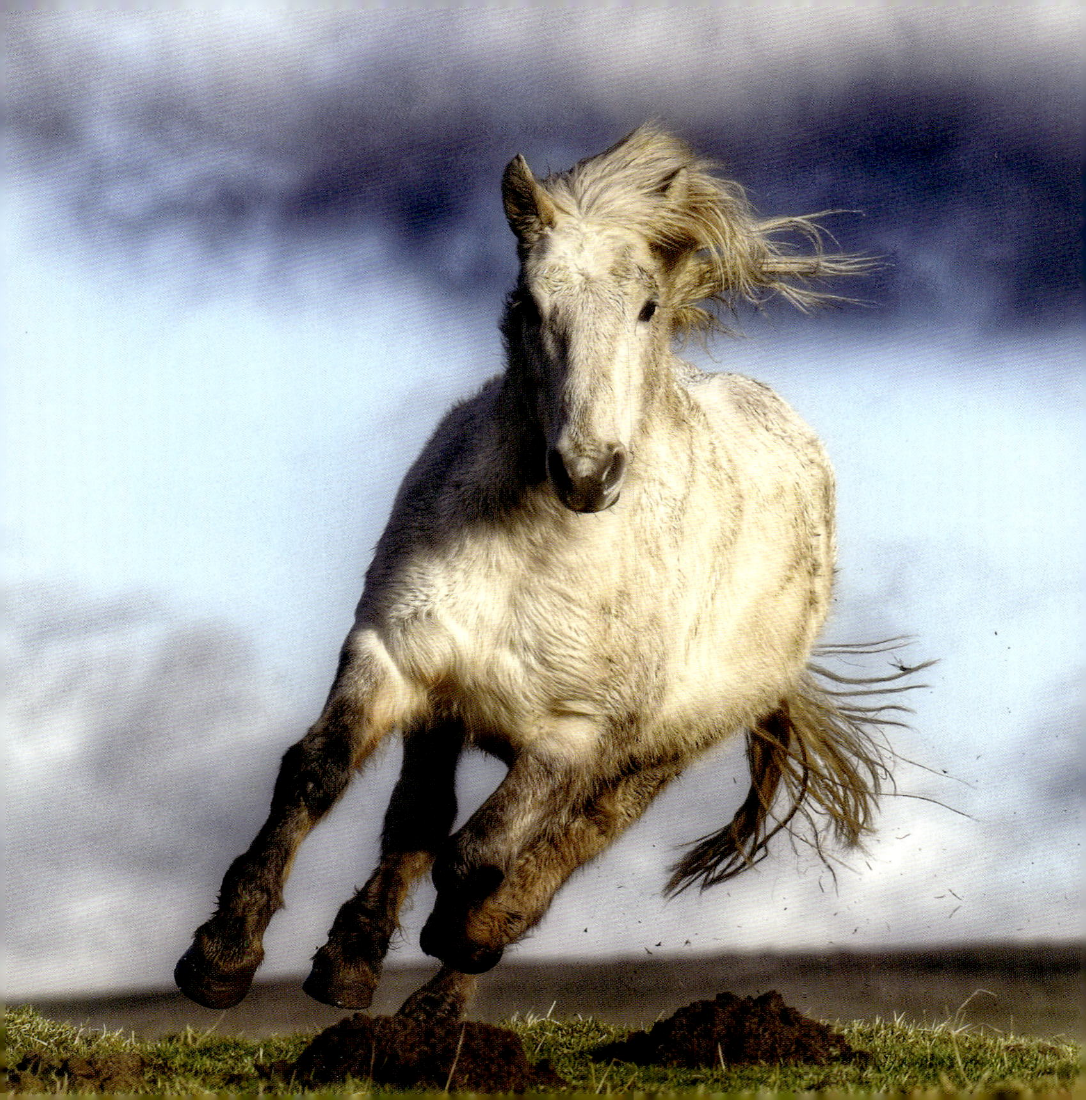

# Highland Pony

There is no doubt that the Highland pony can trace its ancestry back through the mists of antiquity. Jarlshof at Sumburgh on the Shetland mainland, is the oldest continuously inhabited site in Scotland; during the Norse period (9–14th Century) there is evidence that ponies were kept there as bones have been found. The Bressay Stone was discovered on Shetland in 1852 and, dating back to the 9th Century, it depicts a rider mounted on a pony.

The Bressay Stone

**Highland Pony Society**
www.highlandponysociety.com
**Height:** Not to exceed 14.2hh*.
**Colours:** A range of duns: mouse, yellow, grey, and cream. Grey, brown, black, bay, and occasionally liver chestnut with silver mane and tail are also permissible. Dorsal eel stripe is typical but not essential and zebra stripes on the inside of the forelegs, which may fade with age. Foal coat may change from birth to maturity. A small star is acceptable, other white markings are discouraged.

**Characteristics as described by the Highland Pony Society:** Well balanced, compact pony with all its features being in proportion to its height. It is one of the largest of the British Native Breeds and should show substance and strength. Action: straight and free moving without undue knee action.

**Status:** At Risk (500 to 900). *Rare Breeds Survival Trust.*

*hands high is a unique measurement for horses. One hand is equal to 4 inches (10 cm).

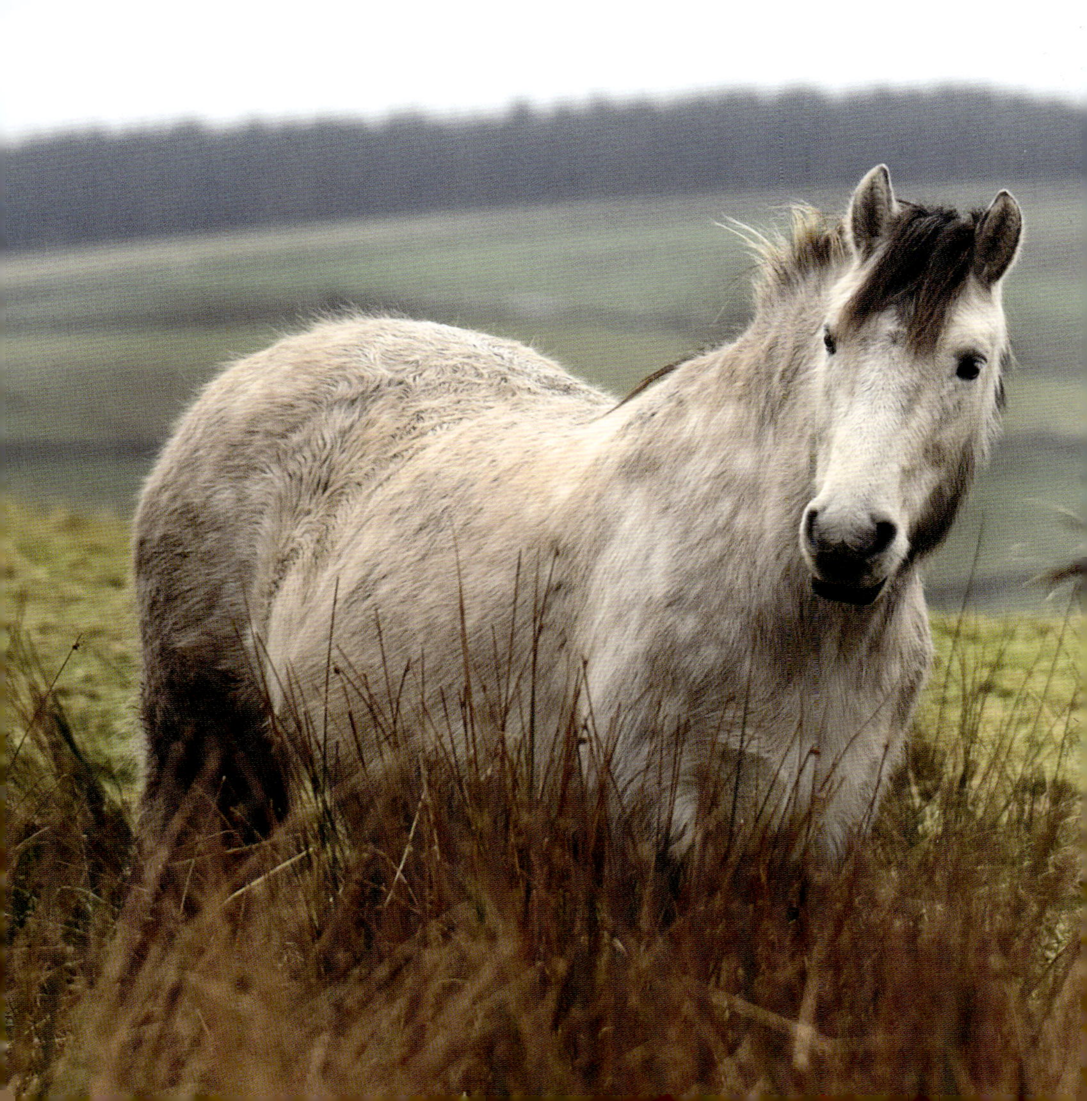

Many places on the mainland have similar stones depicting ponies being used for hunting deer or boar, the rider sometimes depicted with a spear and a round shield, and there is even one depicting a pair of ponies drawing a small chariot. One can deduce that ponies/horses were used for many different tasks both during and after the Roman occupation.

Although all are descended from the same base stock, from the beginning of the 1800s there were two distinct types of Highland pony: the Western Isles and the Mainland. Eleven islands off the westerly coast of Scotland all had their own types of pony. These islands are Arran, Barra, Harris, Islay, Jura, Lewis, Mull, Rhum, Skye, Tiree, and Uist. The individual characteristics of each pony were based on the following:

1. Environment

2. How they were treated within their island community

3. Selection for the specific work required on each island

4. Attempts made at different times during the nineteenth century to 'help' the quality of the animals by breeding. These breeding efforts were not always taken up to any degree by the island inhabitants, as the stallions used were as diverse as an Arab at one end of the scale and a Clydesdale at the other. Simple geography meant that the island ponies were therefore relatively 'pure' until the beginning

of the nineteenth century. However, the Mainland type who, whilst sharing the strength, sure-footedness and docility of its island cousins, developed into a generally larger animal for use in the plough or the cart.

The oldest record of Mainland horse breeding is in the Charter of Kelso. Before AD 1200, Gilbert de Imfraville, Earl of Angus granted the monks of Kelso a tenth of the foals bred in his forest. Subsequently however monarchs were keen to keep equines within their realm. In 1406, James I would only allow animals to be exported if they were at least three years old but by 1567, the reign of James VI, this had moved to no exporting at all. James V passed a law in 1535 to 'increase the size of the Scottish horses' and to this end James' groom, Charles Murray, was sent on a purchasing sortie to Sweden and Denmark. Louis XII sent James a present of a collection of the best French breeds.

In his *Thoroughbreds and other Ponies* (1903) Sir Walter Gilbey states that 'Highland ponies may be divided into three classes.

Firstly, small ponies of Barra and the outer islands, 12.2–13.2hh.

Secondly, the high class riding pony of the Western Highlands and Isles 13.2–14.2hh.

Thirdly, Garrons...a good deal bigger...up to 15hh.

By the early 1930s due to crossbreeding, none of these three distinctive types were still recognised.

We have seen in previous chapters how a war can make a difference to the fortunes of a native breed and so it was with the Highland in the Boer War. Very much seen as a utility horse, these strong, patient, medium-sized ponies were perfect for the war. The Lovat Scouts were mounted on Highland ponies and were the first military unit to wear camouflage or ghillie suits as they were properly known. The Scouts were initially made up of highland estate workers who were crack marksmen, practiced in tracking, stalking, and fieldcraft. They were perfectly matched with their ponies to fight a guerilla war in the bush.

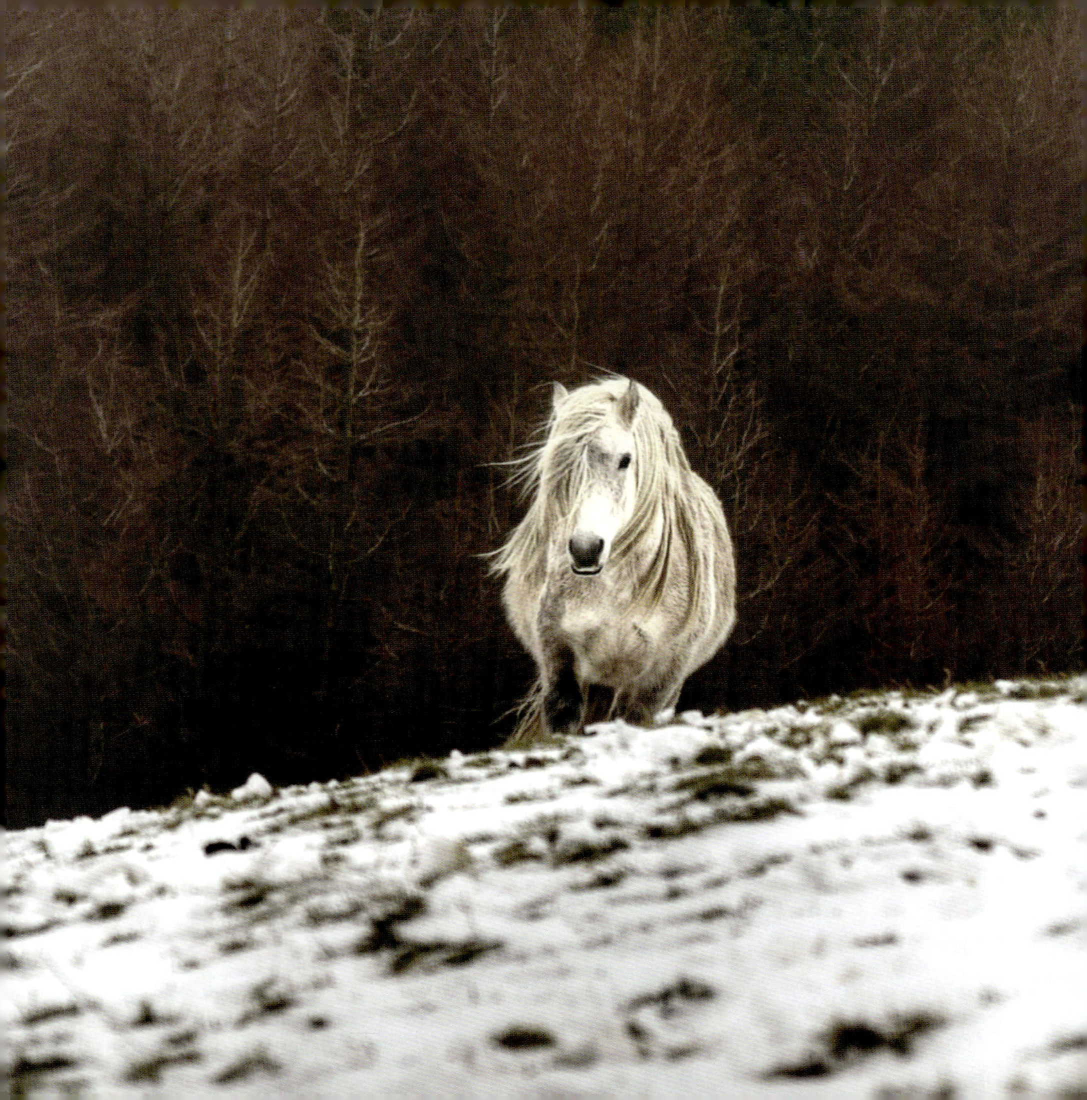

Major the Marquis of Tullibardine raised a Scottish regiment known as Tullibardine's Scottish Horse. It appeared in the army lists of mounted volunteer regiments. Recruited from both Scotland and Caledonian Societies in London and the Commonwealth, it went on to gain a reputation as the best body of men in the South African conflict. Needless to say, those who were actually raised from Scotland brought the Highland pony with them. The Marquis' father, the Duke of Atholl, personally raised 831 men from his area.

The Highland Pony Society was formed in 1923 and only a year later had 64 members. Requests for ponies were coming to the society from mines for pit ponies, to pull vans in cities and as ride-and-drive ponies.

John Stewart-Murray, 8th Duke of Atholl.

Highland Pony

The Highland had a well deserved and worthy reputation as a strong and docile work horse.

Primarily known in Scotland as a ghillie's horse, the Highland pony was used for transporting deer and other game animals down from mountain shoots.

The ghillie pony featured here is used by Jess Fergusson on an estate for bringing culled deer down off the mountain. The culling keeps the deer herds to sustainable numbers for the area they graze and ensures that those remaining are as healthy and strong as possible coming into the winter.

The Native Pony Book

Ewan Ormiston of Caick Forest is credited with starting pony trekking in Scotland at Easter 1952. The Ormistons (father and son) had been asked for suggestions on how to introduce visitors to the countryside and they suggested ponies. The steady Highland pony, with an enormous weight carrying ability for its size and steady but ground-covering paces, was a natural choice for any trekking stable. Today the Highland pony can still be found trekking but can also take on long distance courses, novice cross-country and log hauling or farm work in places inaccessible even to the most agile quad bike or Land Rover. They prefer to live out, irrespective of the weather; their thick double winter coat with a water-shedding topcoat and a warm, finer layer of hair close to the skin helps them

Highland Pony

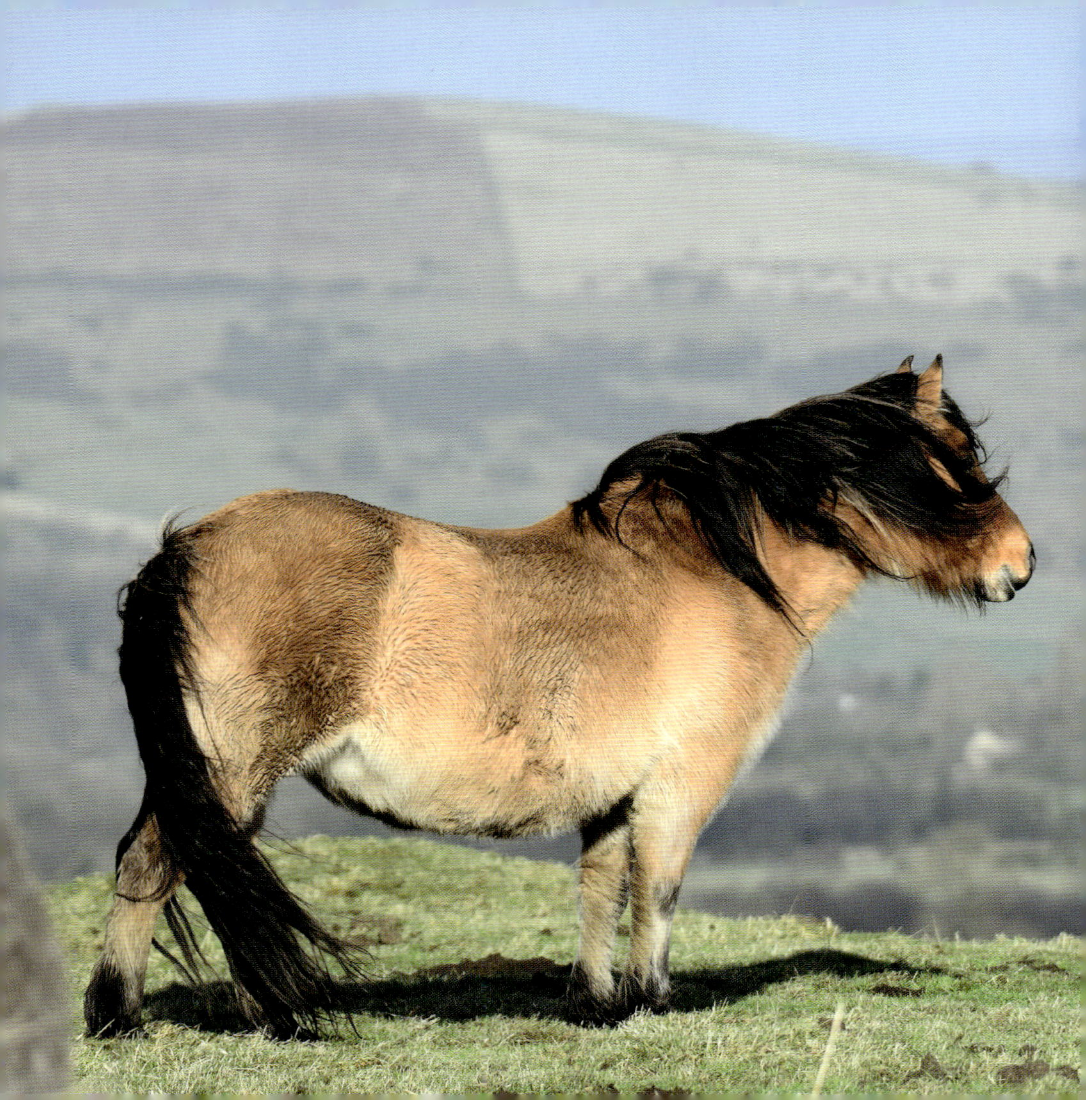

cope with severely inhospitable conditions. The forelock, mane and tail are thick and luxuriant and offer some protection against biting insects in the summer.

The Highland pony is not restricted by subjective assessment of either confirmation or height to pass into the Stud Book. What it must have is a pure Highland pedigree, verified by a DNA test on hair taken at the time of vetting for registration as a stallion for breeding purposes. The only negative criterion for a stallion is that it should have no white markings, these are thought to indicate cross-breeding in the past and are very much discouraged, only a small white star is permissible.

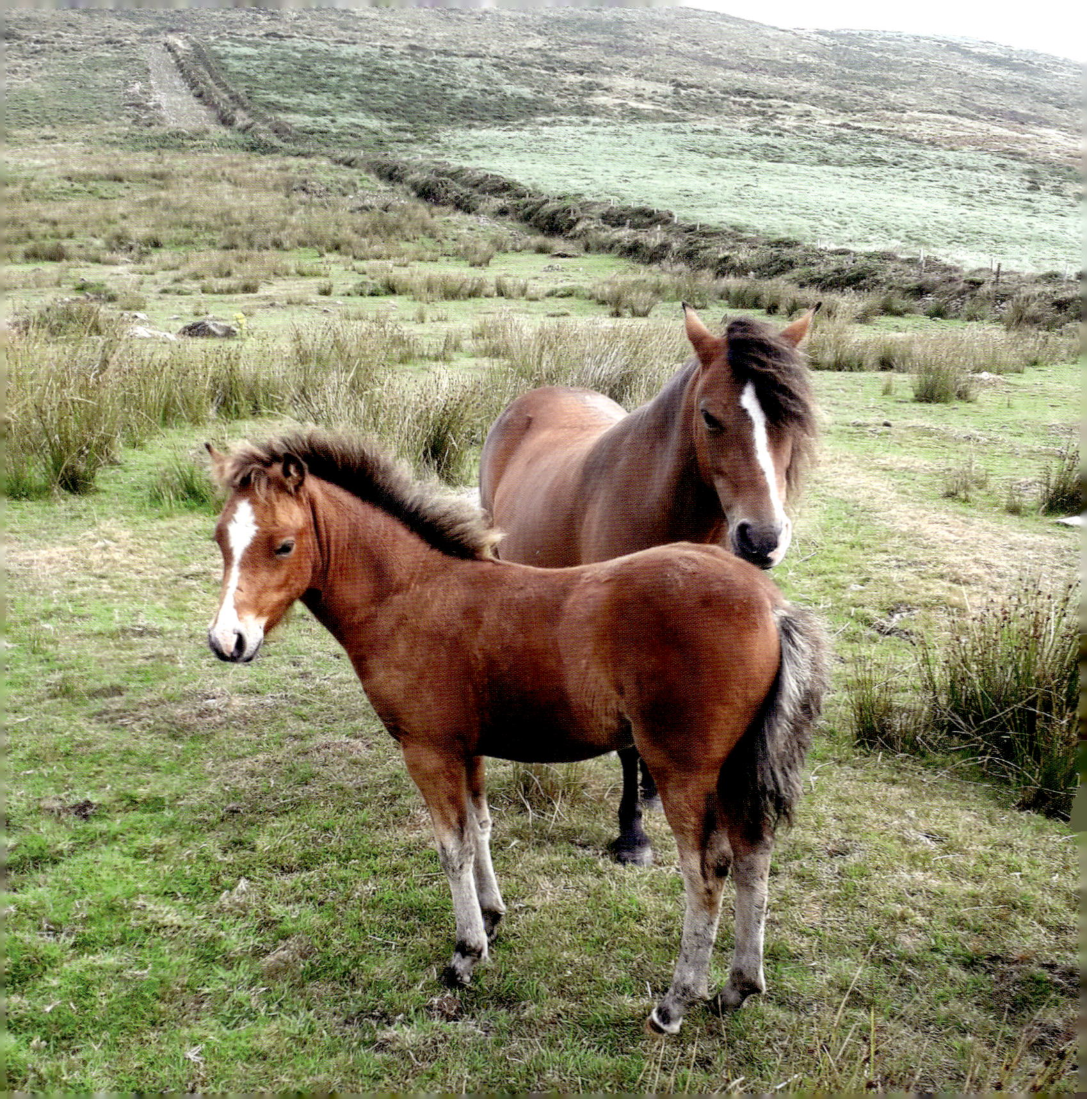

# Kerry Bog Pony

The Kerry Bog pony (KBP) comes from southwestern Ireland and was mainly used for transporting peat from bogs and kelp from the sea to small villages. After work it would be turned out to fend for itself. It is a strong, resilient pony known for its ability to survive in harsh conditions. It has a low weight-to-height ratio, which makes it ideal for moving across soft and undulating bogs. Whilst having clean strong legs, it has a noticeably short cannon bone, with a short pastern too and rather upright, hard, tough hooves that rarely need trimming. Its lowly background and simple domestic uses mean that the KBP has passed almost unnoticed through the landscape of its native area. At several points in its history it was virtually extinct but has somehow managed to cling on and survive.

**The Kerry Bog Pony Cooperative Society**
www.kerrybogpony.ie

**Height:** Mares 10–11hh, stallions/geldings 11–12hh*.

**Colours:** Brown or brownish black, but bay, chestnut, grey and dun are also found. Coloured ponies do not meet the Breed Standard and will be placed in Class 3 on inspection.

**Characteristics as described by The Kerry Bog Pony Cooperative Society:** The KBP is a powerful pony with good bone and great weight and strength relative to its size. This, together with its excellent conformation gives the pony a lovely straight and level action with good balance. Whilst kind, sensible, confident and well mannered, it also possesses great courage and endurance.

**Status:** Not currently accredited as a rare breed. *Rare Breeds Survival Trust.*

*hands high is a unique measurement for horses. One hand is equal to 4 inches (10 cm).

The traditional uses of the KBP continued into the 1960s, when they were still used for dairy deliveries and turf collection from the bog to the roadside. However, gradually as we have seen with other native breeds, their uses were overtaken by a more mechanical life and they began what could have been their final decline. In the 1990s in Glenbeigh, Co Kerry, the landlord of The Red Fox Inn, John Mulvihill, grew interested in what had happened to the ponies he had seen regularly in his youth and began to do some research. John found that numbers were very low, so he gathered a small herd around Glenbeigh and into his Kerry Bog Village nearby.

Despite sterling support from Daniel Hutch, a local vet, John had difficulty making progress alone. He had decided that the Kerry Bog Pony should be the descriptive name of the breed and so he put his information about this tiny population out to the media. Soon a KBP stallion called Flashy Fox was to be seen on RTÉ, Ireland's National Television broadcaster, and this is where Weatherbys Blood Typing and DNA Laboratory at the Irish Equine Centre came in. Dr John Flynn of Weatherbys saw the small pony with the wonderful conformation and contacted John Mulvihill, offering to blood- and DNA-type his little herd to see if the KBP was in fact a separate breed. The Kerry Bog pony is now characterised at a genetic level and identified as a distinct breed.

Genetic testing continues on all registered KBPs and this has helped to build a full picture of the background of the breed. It would seem that however unlikely it appears, the KBP is genetically closer to the Welsh pony than the

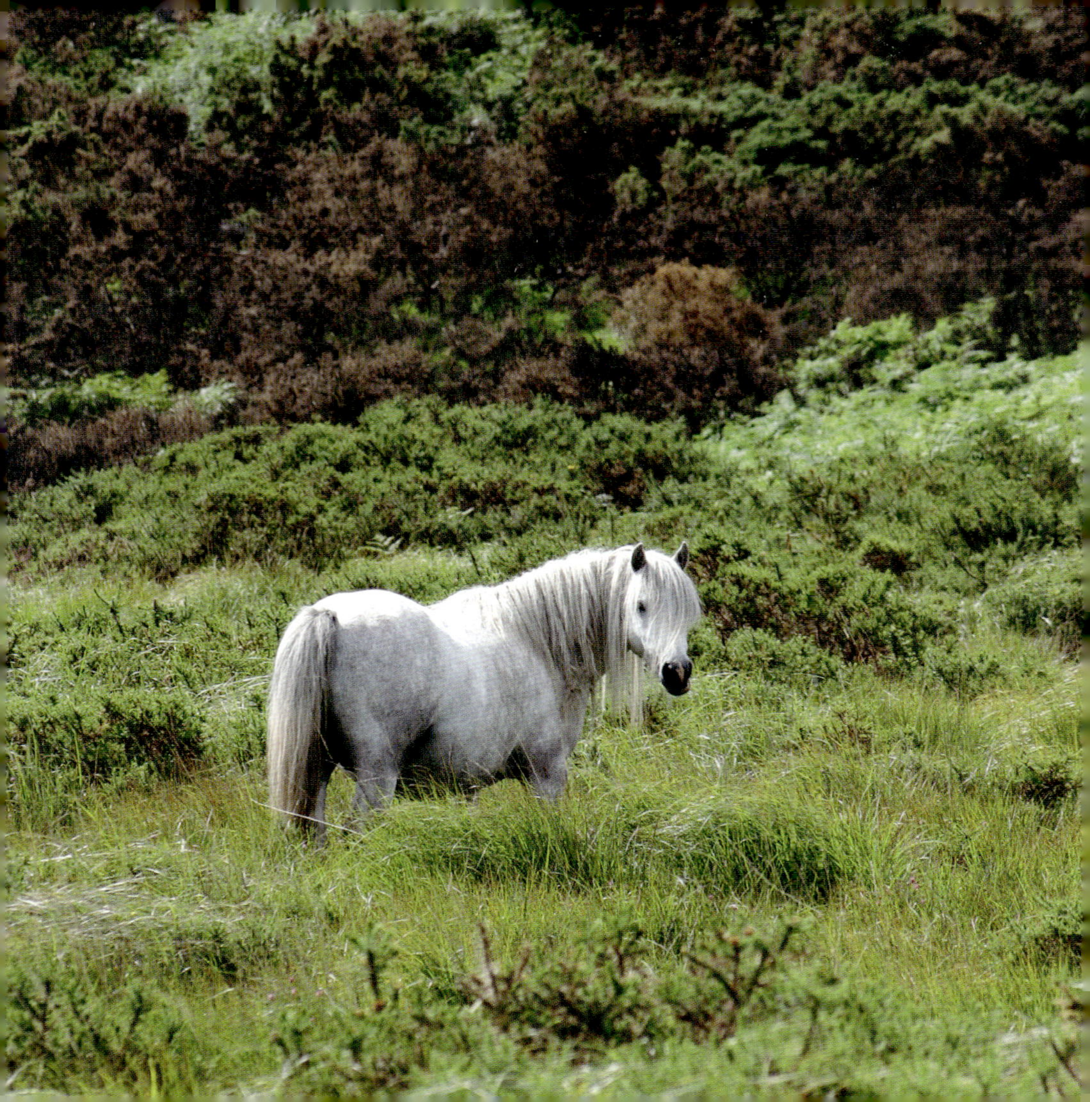

Connemara from the same island. The genetic make-up of the Kerry Bog pony is linked to pony breeds in the more northern regions of Europe and Scandinavia.

One can only hypothesise that these links indicate a connection to the Viking invasions of Ireland between 795 AD and 1000 AD. Historically we know that the Vikings transported ponies. In light of this, it would seem quite possible that ponies went to Ireland and/or were carried back to Europe.

Once he had gathered his herd, John Mulvihill was encouraged by both Daniel Hutch and Dr. Leo Curran, the Irish native breeds specialist, to keep precise and accurate records of the pedigrees and relationships of the KBPs. This would control inbreeding, form an historical basis for the breed and indicate if certain lines caused problems to confirmation or temperament. From these very small beginnings the Kerry Bog Pony Society was formed.

1995 saw Timothy Clifford MVB, MRCVS writing a breed standard from the known herd and at the first AGM of The Kerry Bog Pony Co-operative Society Ltd in 2005, this standard was unanimously adopted. Passports for KBPs are now issued by Horse Sport Ireland.

The Kerry Bog pony today excels in every situation where an intelligent, strong, well-balanced pony can excel. In hand, ridden and driven, they have proved their worth to those searching for the perfect family pony and are much valued on the island of Ireland and now across the globe.

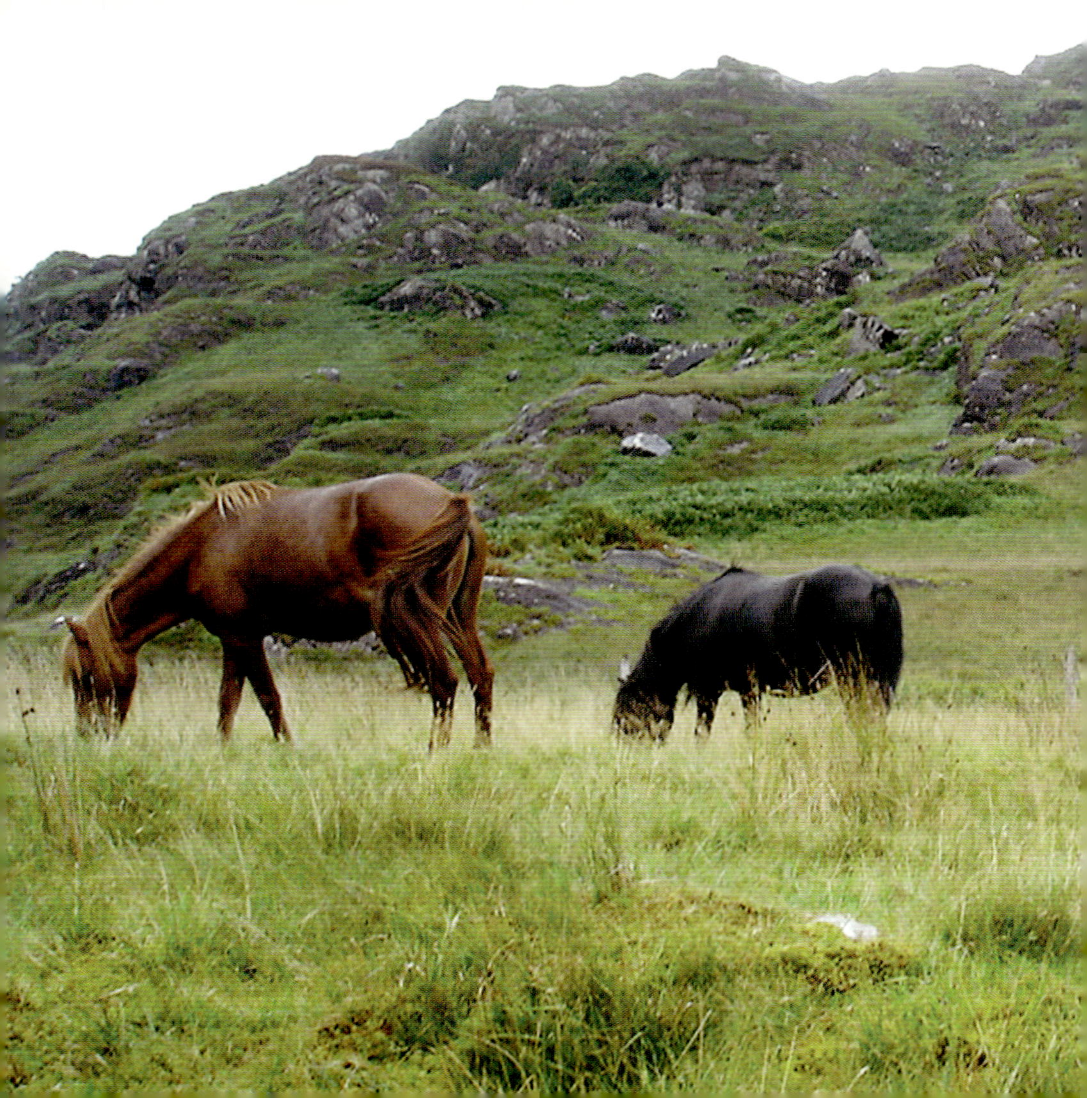

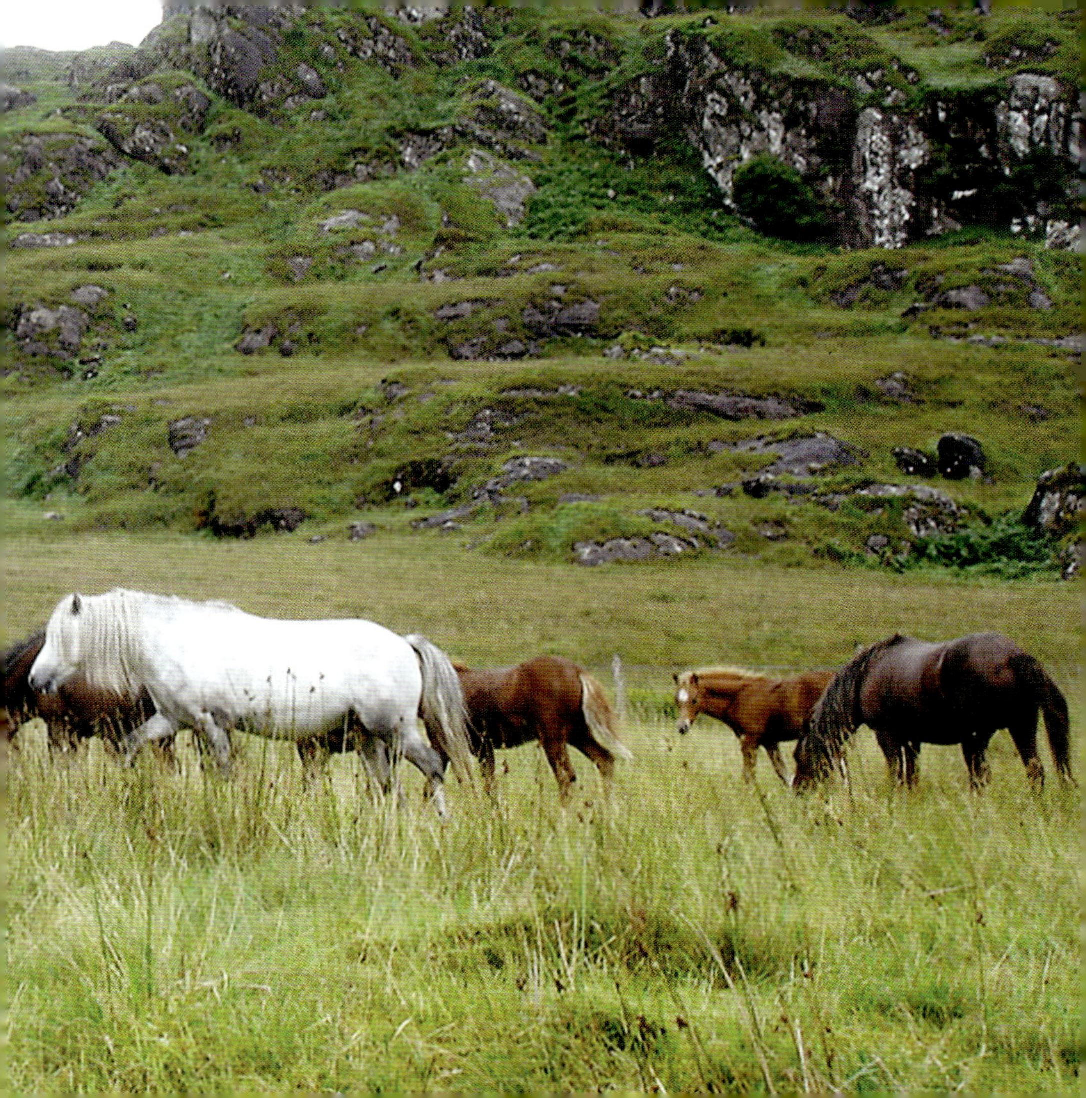

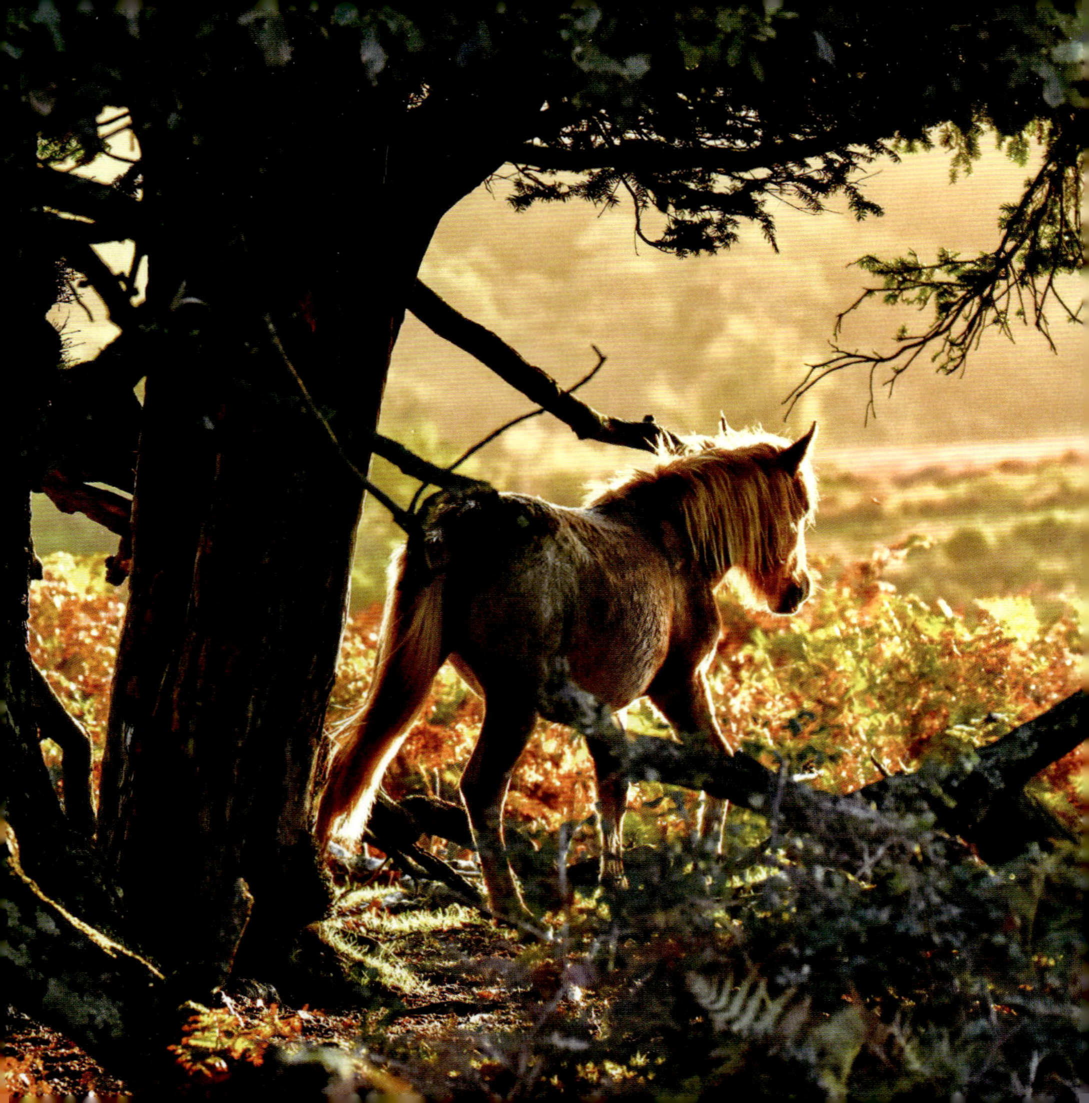

# New Forest Pony

**New Forest Pony Breeding & Cattle Society**
www.newforestpony.com

**Height:** No minimum stated but usually not less than 12hh, maximum height 14.2hh*.

**Colours:** Any colour except piebald, skewbald, spotted or blue-eyed cream. There are complex genetic standards for certain colours, mainly grey and cream that may be found on the website of New Forest Pony Breeding & Cattle Society in the Breed Description section. White markings are only permitted on the head or lower limbs below the knee on the forelegs and the hock on the back legs.

**Characteristics as described by the New Forest Pony Breeding & Cattle Society:** Of working type with substance. They should have sloping shoulders, strong quarters, plenty of flat bone, good depth of body, straight limbs and good hard round feet. The ponies are quite capable of carrying adults, while narrow enough for small children. The smaller ponies, though not up to so much weight, often show more quality. Action should be free, active and straight, but not exaggerated. The New Forest pony has an amenable temperament that generally makes it very suitable for multiple disciplines.

**Status:** At Risk (500 to 900). *Rare Breeds Survival Trust.*

*hands high is a unique measurement for horses. One hand is equal to 4 inches (10 cm).

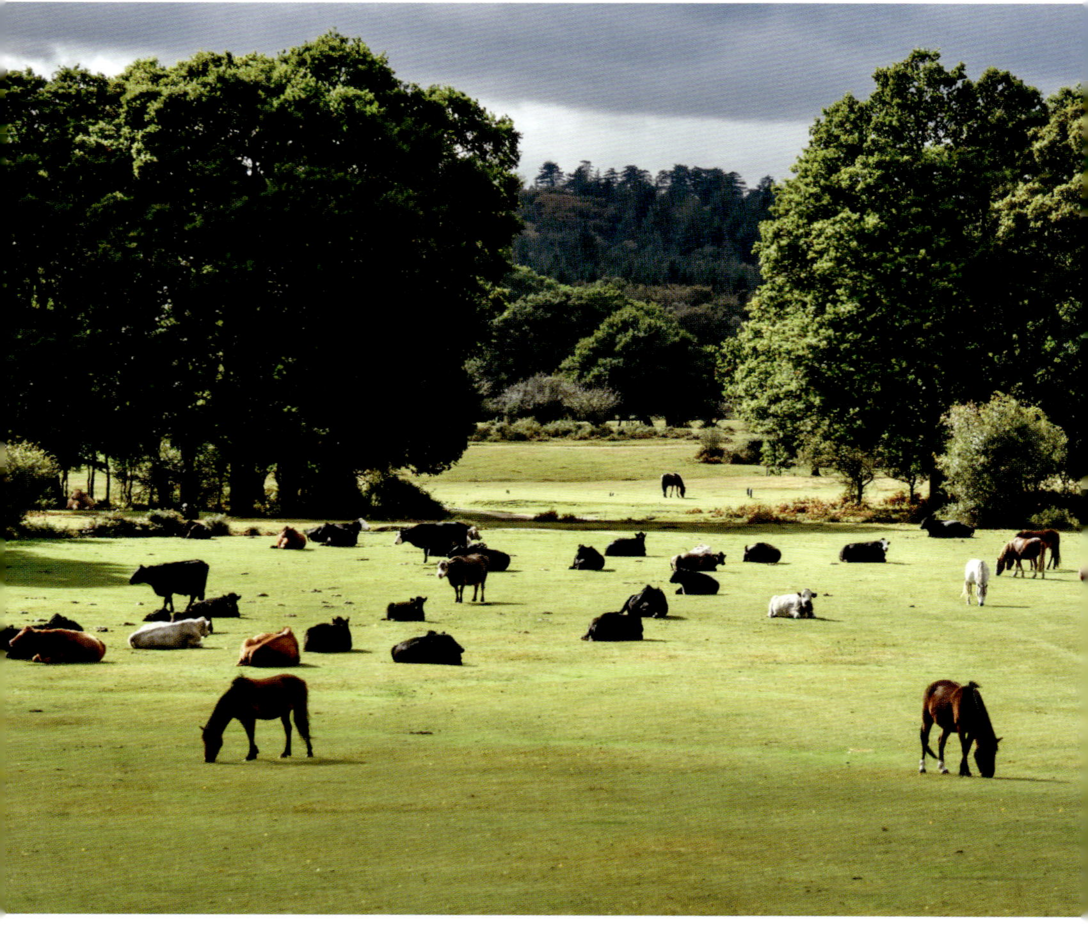

The native pony depicted in the Bayeux Tapestry was probably seized in or around Hastings and could conceivably have been a New Forest pony. In the time of King Canute (1017-1035) there is mention of wild horses living in the forest. By 1217, the forest pony population had grown large enough for it to be considered an annual revenue source for the Crown. In March of that year, Henry III gave the benefit of this income (accrued during the annual pony droves) to the monks of Beaulieu until November 1220. This largesse was offered for the benefit of the soul of his late father, King John.

The New Forest pony (NFP) has been subjected to some improvement strategies over the centuries, with varying degrees of success. In 1765 a Dorset farmer bought a thoroughbred stallion for a pittance at a knock down sale at Tattersalls of Newmarket. The stallion, named Marske, was not allowed to run on the forest but did cover selected mares in the area for the fee of half a guinea. In his book "Thoroughbred and Other Ponies" (1903) Sir Walter Gilbey states "For four years at least, the New Forest breed of ponies were being improved by the very best Thoroughbred blood, the effects of which continued to be apparent for many years after Marske had left the district." Perhaps most noteworthy in the historical sense amongst the 'improvements', was when in 1852 Queen Victoria loaned an Arab stallion, Zorah, to stand at stud for several years. He was not used much by the commoners who owned the NFPs and his influence was therefore slight and the degeneration of the breed continued.

Decades passed. It should be explained that those deriving a livelihood from breeding ponies could buy a cheap, tired old mare; as long as they had commoner's rights they could then release her to run on the forest. With luck they would have a youngster the following year, which could be sold on at a profit and with little work on the part of the human. The value of the ponies fell at the local horse fairs, always a clear indication of how buyers felt about their quality. Four well-bred stallions were bought in but, as their offspring were most often sold on, they too did nothing to raise the calibre of the animals running wild.

In 1888, Lord Arthur Cecil, that well-documented champion of the native pony, tried his hand at improvement. From his estate he sent down Black Galloways, of the type mentioned in the Fell and Dale chapters, to try and aid the quality of the base 'Forester' stock. Raising the quality of the Foresters did not really take hold until finally, in 1889, it was deemed necessary to offer an inducement in the form of stallion premiums at a show in April of each year. Winners of the premiums would run on the Forest until August and thus benefit the wild mares running there too.

This scheme did indeed begin to improve the stock and Queen Victoria tried to help again in 1889 with two more Arab stallions; these stood, one for two seasons and the other for three, but neither 'ran' on the forest so the usual problem applied. However, the son of one of these stallions, out of a Welsh mare, stood in the district and became very popular with commoners.

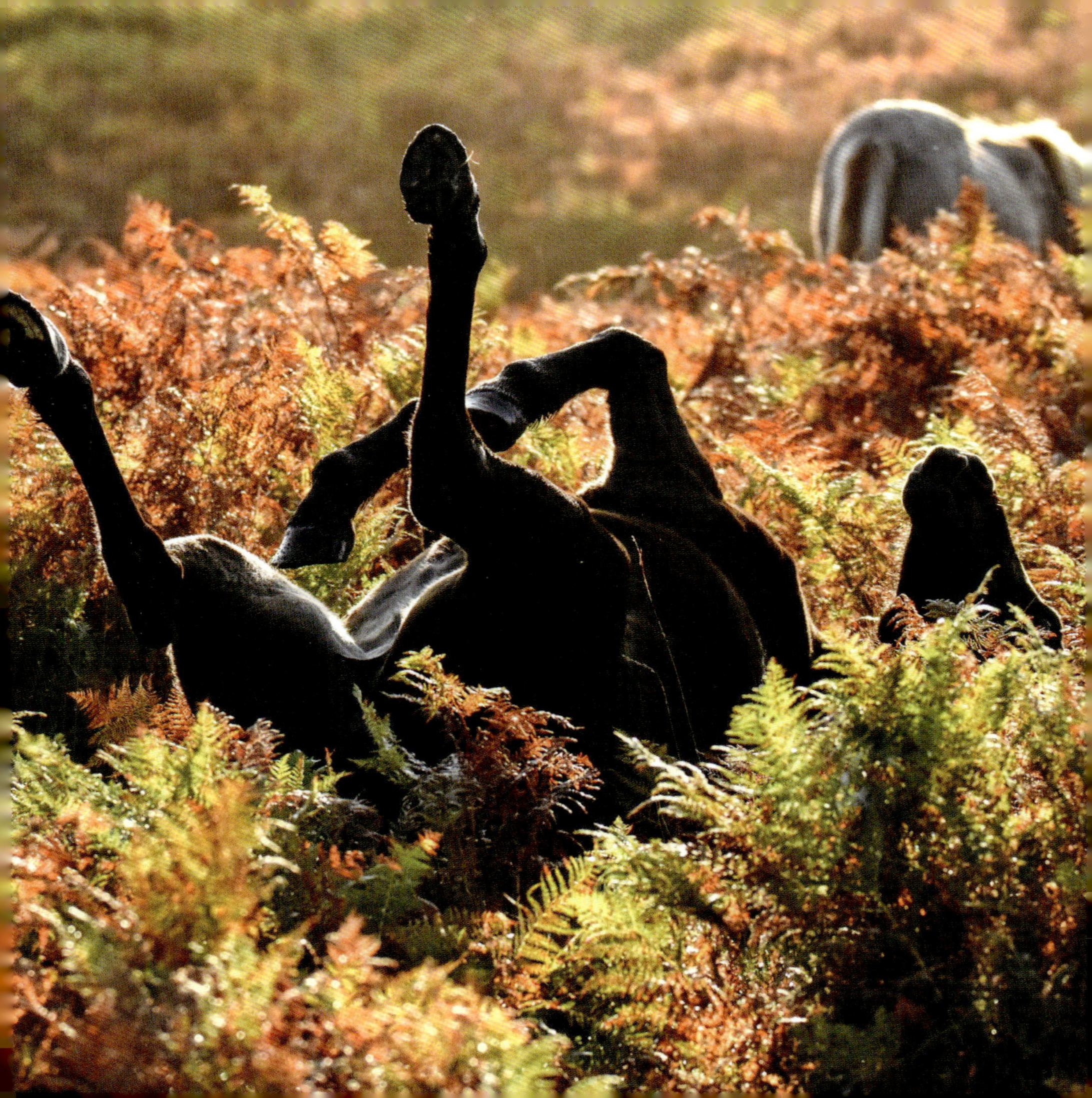

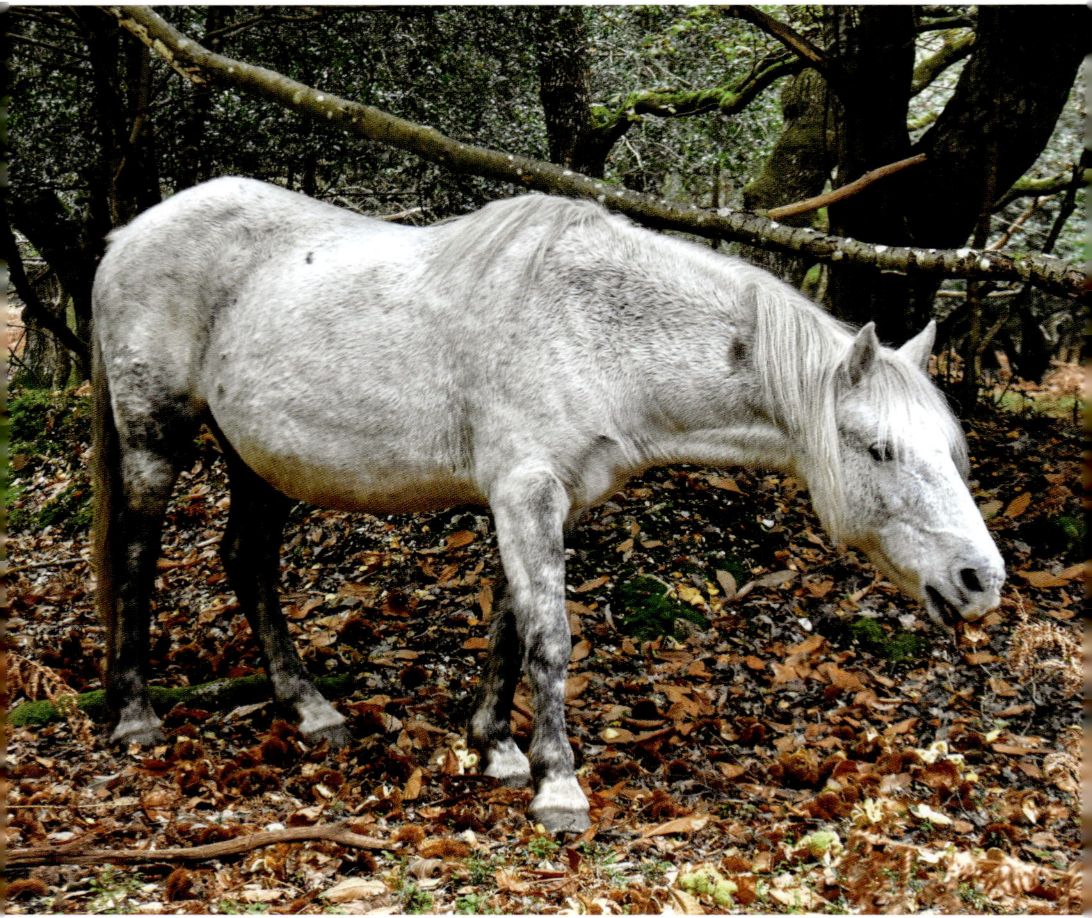

Gradually the calibre of the Foresters began to improve and The Association for the Improvement of The Breed of New Forest Ponies was formed in 1891. This move was enthusiastically supported by the Verderers (the administrators and controllers of the stallions within the forest's land) and several well-connected supporters of the breed including the ever-influential Lord Arthur Cecil. The formation of this group encouraged commoners to think ahead and keep their best colt youngsters as the stallions of the future, rather than selling them on. To this end and with some financial help from the Board of Agriculture, a raft of premiums and prizes was offered. An annual stallion show was held in April at Lyndhurst and the Verderers acted as inspectors and awarded the prizes.

The Burley and District New Forest Pony and Cattle Society came into being in 1906 with a much more ambitious agenda. Firstly to create a register of New Forest ponies belonging to the society and secondly to create a matching premium scheme for mares as that which had been originated for stallions. By 1910 the first stud book appeared with 118 stallions and 356 mares. Each animal registered had details of colour, foal year, owners, breeders, breeding, prizes gained and the area (known as a 'haunt') where each animal ran and in which year. The brand mark for each group of ponies was listed too.

1899 had seen the first proper Mountain & Morland groups entered in the Stud Book and Lord Arthur Cecil's report of 1912 recommended that a special offer, of up to a four year premium for filly foals be instituted for the New Forest pony, to encourage owners to retain breeding stock. New bloodlines from other mountain and moorland breeds were added over time and Fell, Dale, Highland, Dartmoor, and Exmoor are all represented in the early stud books.

We have seen before how the native breeds took to the battlefields during conflicts, seeing action during the Boar War and the First World War and the Foresters were no exception. Their strength, sure-footedness and calm temperament were of great help to the Forest Scouts in South Africa and in France during WWI.

In 1938, the two foundation groups, The Association and The Society consolidated, to form the New Forest Pony Breeding and Cattle Society (NFPBCS), the body which still holds the Stud Book of Origin today. Since the turn of the 20th Century, no alien stallions have been allowed to roam and the breed continues to breed very true to type.

All the ponies seen on the forest are owned by commoners who have 'The Rights of Common Pasture' and may graze ponies, cattle and pigs. The welfare of these animals and the administrative control of the stallions is the responsibility of the Verderers in the Forest Court. With its five elected members and five state appointees (DEFRA, Forestry Commission, etc.) it meets once a month to consider matters concerning the running of the forest. The Verderers employ five agisters who act in their specific area to support the animals, the commoners, the forest and people moving through the forest. They are on 24hr call and attend traffic incidents involving animals where they care for the injured, advise of breach of byelaws, arrange pony and cattle drives and generally patrol and oversee the workings of the forest lands.

Whilst its range is large (approx 90,000 acres) in south-west Hampshire and south-east Wiltshire, grazing for the NFP is generally sparse and poor. The ponies tend to gather in 'haunts' often where they were foaled. Herds grow within families. Mares stay out all year but some stallions are only on the forest

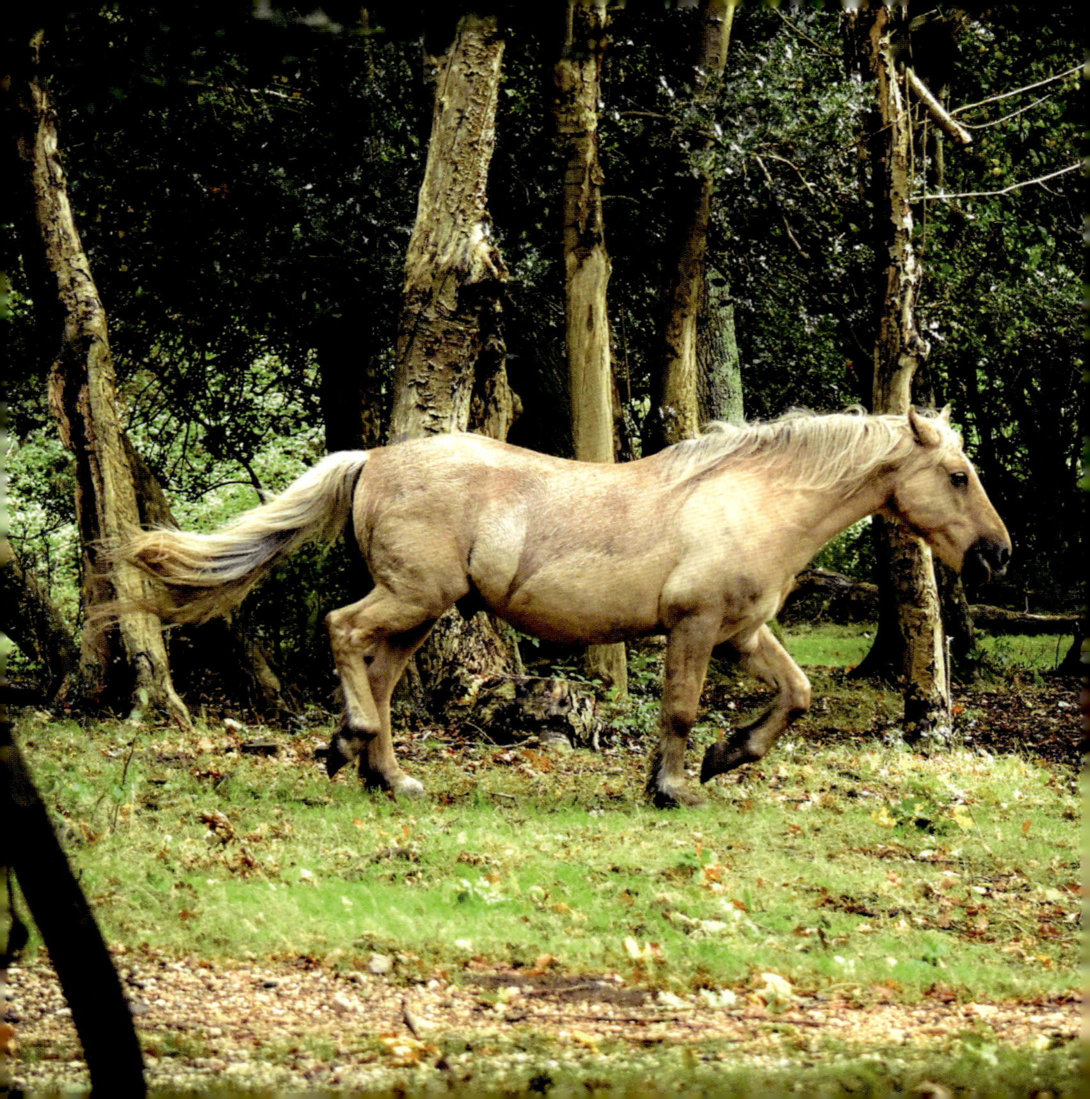

from May to September/October. The valley bottoms offer some good grass but are dotted with bogs. These can prove dangerous in the spring to ponies hunting for the first fresh shoots and the agisters and owners have to keep a watchful eye out for ponies caught by them. The bogs do however offer water grasses, sedges and rushes for the ponies and the struggle to find food has made them resourceful to the point of eating acorns, even though most of them cannnot take many. Young, fresh leaves of oak and beech are taken too, along with gorse, heather and brambles.

As the tallest native breed, the New Forest pony is considered the perfect 'family pony' as it can be ridden comfortably by both children and adults. Its familiarity with roads and all forms of traffic makes it a truly bombproof ride and drive. Sure-footedness is a given in a pony raised regularly moving through high heather and gorse heath, free-pathed woodland, and rabbit warrens. The NFPBCS holds a New Forest Performance Pony of the Year Competition, which covers every riding discipline from dressage to driving and eventing to endurance. A minimum of two different events are to be scored towards the various trophies and it underlines the scope which can be covered by this most versatile of native breeds and proves that quality certainly has been maintained.

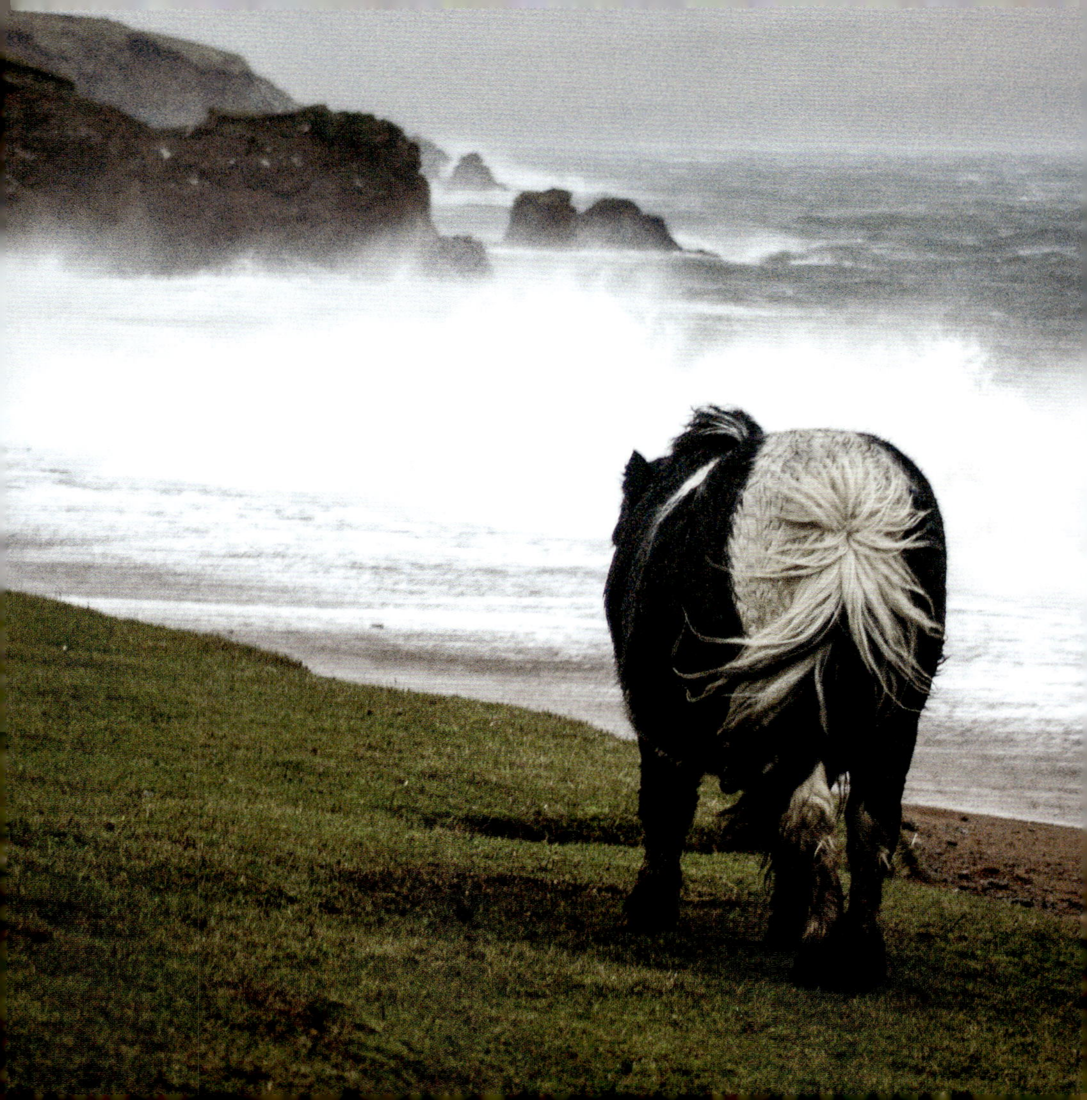

# Shetland Pony

Shetland is not just one island in the far north of Scotland; it is a group of approximately 100, with a population of about 23,000 people spread over 16 inhabited islands. It is in the north Atlantic and, if you look on a map, it is as close to Norway as it is to Aberdeen on the north-east coast of Scotland. The largest island is always referred to as The Mainland, not to be confused with the Scottish mainland.

It is possible that the Viking hoards touched Shetland as early as A.D. 700 and it would seem that some of these Norsemen settled on the islands. Wild ponies of a Shetland type had run the moors of Caithness and Orkney as well as Shetland since the time of the split of the islands from the near continent. These wild ponies are thought to have their beginnings in ponies from the tundra

**The Shetland Pony Stud-Book Society**
www.shetlandponystudbooksociety.co.uk

**Height:** Not exceeding 10.5hh*.

**Colours:** Any colour is acceptable, except spotted.

**Characteristics as described by the Shetland Pony Society:** The Shetland pony has a general air of vitality (presence), stamina and robustness. Two types established within the breed... the heavier-boned draught animal with powerful chest and shoulders for driving and the lighter free-moving pony with high tail carriage and pretty head for riding. Their docile nature is ideal for a child's first pony and they can hold their own amongst much larger ponies. They are driving ponies par excellence and for their size they are the strongest of all the horse breeds.

*hands high is a unique measurement for horses. One hand is equal to 4 inches (10 cm).

(approx. 13.2hh) and the mountains (approx. 12.2hh) of southern Europe. We know the neolithic tribes of Sumburgh had eaten them, as bone evidence has been found.

The first Norsemen settlers were fishermen and did not bring horses with them but they did have experience of equines. Native ponies could well have been used to carry nets to the boats and catch back up to encampments.

The Norse translation of the word viking is "freebooting voyage, piracy". The next use of the islands was as a base for Norse pirates. From Shetland they could set off to pillage down the west coast of Scotland and thence on to Ireland. They had no real need for the ponies as they were simply moving cargo from one ship to another. The Norsemen who settled on the islands used names from their home and their pirate past is still to be found on Shetland in the place names.

In the middle of the ninth century, Shetland came under full Norwegian rule, with the Earl of Orkney as administrator on behalf of King Harald Hairfair. The pirates were cleared out and whilst there was no need to use ponies to do this, boats being the more usual means of transport, the Shetland pony was still used for 'crofting'. The chores of peat-carrying to keep the fires burning and other smallholding tasks made them useful day-to-day. At this time ponies were fewer on the mainland of Scotland than they were on Shetland, probably because the larger animals found it harder to survive through a hard winter. The Shetland ponies of this period were known for their ability to sustain on a very poor diet, often quoted as "cods heads and seaweed" and so a trade in these small tough ponies began. The exporters of ponies to Faeroe or Iceland did not have to ship them nearly as far as those coming from Norway and so the activity thrived.

The remoteness of the Shetland Isles kept the ponies safe from any historical oddities wrought in the British Isles during the following centuries. Henry VIII's Act 32 of 1541 as outlined in the Carneddau chapter did not touch the north of Scotland and it was not until 1604 and the Stuart period that once again the Shetland pony became a point of interest. The Shetlanders had only just stopped transacting public business in Norwegian when the first ruling in English was recorded in the Court Book of Scalloway. It concerned the removal or 'wrongeous gripster' of twenty-one horses and mares. In this instance, these animals were Shetland ponies. Up to this point ponies had been considered virtually public property until, in 1612, all inhabitants of the islands were forbidden by law to ride another man's horse on payment of a fine. Grazing rights were also prescribed and no animal was permitted to graze the hill pastures between 1st June and the time of the harvest, on pain of being apprehended.

It has been suggested at various times in their history, that Shelties (as the Islanders call them) are small because of poor grazing and extreme living conditions in the north Atlantic. This is not however, born out by the fact that, given an easier, better-fed life in the south of the country, pure bred ponies breed no taller. They are small by nature's design and are not stunted in growth. The Shetland pony confirmation has everything in proportion. Perhaps it should be said that instead of their smallness being as a result of poor feeding, their very smallness is how they could survive on a poor diet.

There is a wonderful description of the Shetland pony in Rev. John Brand's Brief Description of Orkney, Zetland, Pightland-Firth and Caithness (1701) 'They have a sort of little horses called Shelties... they are of less size than the Orkney Horses, for some will be but 9 or 10 handbreaths high...although so small yet are they full of vigour and life...some, whom an able man can lift up in his arms, yet will they carry him and a woman behind him 8 miles forward and as many back.' William Youatt, the vet and animal welfare writer also wrote of them, 'The Shetland pony called in Scotland a Sheltie ... is often exceedingly beautiful, with a small head, good tempered countenance ... legs flat and fine and pretty round feet. These ponies possess immense strength for their size.'

This strength was to be their success and in 1847, following a prohibition Act of Parliament, woman and children were replaced by Shetland ponies in the pits of the north of England. The demand for the ponies increased as did their value and estimates have up to 500 ponies entering the pits every year.

In 1870, Lord Londonderry, the Irish peer who had always shown an interest in Shelties, rented grazing on two islands, Bressay and Noss and established a Shetland stud. He bought the very best stock from all over the islands and began breeding in a thorough and managed way to create the perfect pit pony for his colliaries in Co. Durham. The formula for the perfect 'Londonderry pony' was "as much weight as possible and as near the ground as it can be got". His stallion Jack 16, was the bedrock of the stud and by thirty years of carefully selected close breeding, the very best qualities for a pit pony came to the fore, without any of the defects of confirmation sometimes seen in the ordinary Island ponies. Londonderry also had a stud at Seaham Harbour Co. Durham. To indicate how important he was, when Seaham Harbour closed, Jack himself, his three sons, eight grandsons and one great-grandson, produced 444 foals entered for sale, with only 46 included who were wholly unrelated to him.

The Londonderry Kellas Stud did have great influence on the breed. Its favoured upright shoulder, and lack of withers at the top is perfect

Ponies to the mainland, 1900s.

for a pit pony pulling a heavy cart underground but not as good for a child's riding pony. This last is important as, although only stallions and geldings went underground, the Sheltie began to be popular elsewhere in the UK and USA; their potential as a first pony for children is an obvious selling point. Back on the Islands however, the Shetland pony population began to dip. There were an estimated 10,000 ponies in 1822, by 1870 4,850 and by 1890 only 4,050.

More than a century has passed since the Londonderry Stud was 'improving' the Shetland pony. Following the closure of the Londonderry Studs, other famous Shetland studs bought stallions and mares and close-bred through their own lines. Most of these were in Scotland, The Bruces of Sumburgh, The Mansons of Bressay, Maryfield and Mainland and the Transy Stud of Dunfermine. The stud at Uyeasound on Unst had been going for many years before the Londonderry ponies rose to dominance and they were virtually untouched by the Jack 16 characteristics. They in turn influenced The Earlshall Stud in Dunfermline. Of English studs perhaps The Ladies E & D Hope's South Park Stud in Sussex is the most famous.

There are two important firsts in the background of the Shetland pony. They were the first breed to have a breed society and the first breed to have a stud book. From these early beginnings every dip and weave of their path to the modern pony has been well documented. Formed in 1890, it is perhaps unsurprising that the Marquis of Londonderry was the first President of The Shetland Pony Stud-Book Society (SPS-BS). When the first stud book was published a year later, 409 mares and 48 stallions were registered.

In 1897 the Board of Agriculture for Scotland started a stallion scheme, similar to that started for other native breeds described in this book. Nine stallions were offered for covering the mares of the island crofters. It was a rather hit and miss enterprise as there was little regulation of quality of either stallion or mare and it finally closed when funding was withdrawn in 1932.

After the Depression and two world wars, the 1950s were a marked low point for ponies on Shetland. Canada and the USA showed a surge of interest in Shelties and the islands breeding stock grew thin. However, a Department of Agriculture for Scotland employee called James Dean rode to the rescue. With approval from his superiors, he reinstituted the stallion scheme closed in 1932, to the few areas discovered with any mares. Finally in 1956, The Shetland Pony Stud-Book Society (SPS-BS) agreed that the scheme was of merit and twelve quality stallions went to run on twelve grazings thought to be the most useful. The running of the scheme was handed to the SPS-BS, with the Department retaining approval rights on the stallions and their grazing areas.

To eliminate an issue with non-approved stallions running on the scattalds, (commons) in 1955 the Crofters Act established that only registered and pedigree stallions would be allowed. The inspection of both mares and offspring took a considerable amount of work by Mrs. Betty Cox and the stud book was finally closed in 1972. Mrs Cox was later a President of the SPS-BS.

An annual show and pony sale started in October 1958 and, although initially half-hearted about it, the crofters soon realised that it was a great opportunity to sell on young stock rather than over-winter them. Autumn sales are still carried out annually in Lerwick to this day. In 1971 the Pony Breeders of Shetland Association came into being. The aim of the Association "is to improve communications amongst island breeders in Shetland.

We encourage projects which can improve the quality of Shetland's ponies, and to promote them within the Islands and world-wide." Their improvement schemes, one for stallions and one for fillies and colts, whilst no longer in operation have given the breed a quality legacy still found in the animals of today.

The Shetland as a breed is internationally popular, with a particularly strong following in the Netherlands. Its versatility both under saddle and in harness, and the size of its character, which is totally disproportionate to its physical size, mean that it has a big fan base around the world. With over 100 breeders on the islands of Shetland, it seems unlikely that this diminutive but perfectly formed equine will disappear any day soon.

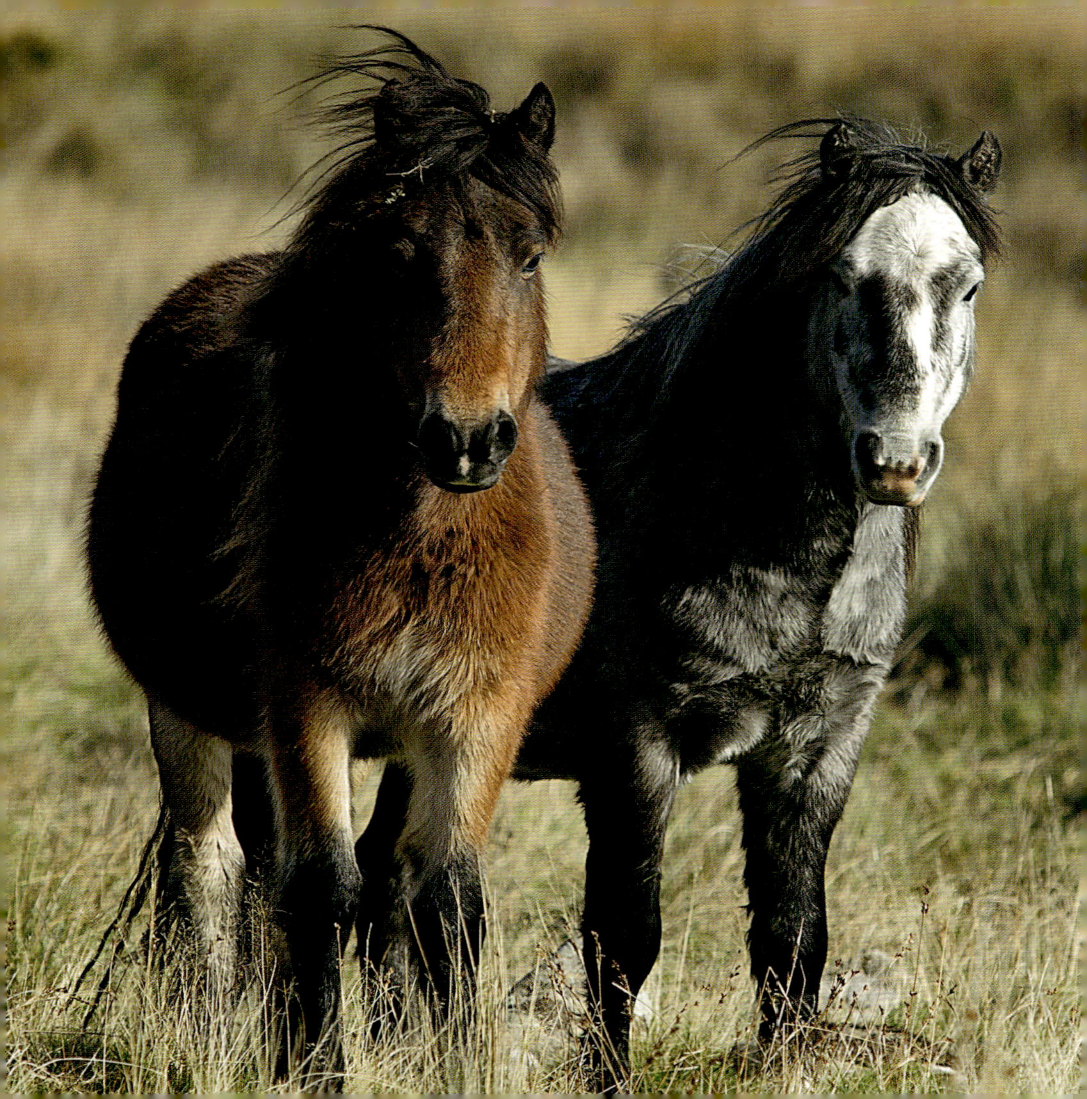

# Welsh Mountain Pony

The baseline history of the Welsh Mountain pony (WMP) is comparatively simple but the development of the breed as we know it today is rather complicated.

The WMP has a truly indigenous ancestry and is often described as the most beautiful of the mountain and moorland breeds. As we have seen throughout this book, the nature of the landscape and climatic influences advises the qualities of its ponies. Their intelligence, soundness, and ability to endure in all adversity are common to all the native ponies and the Welsh Mountain pony is no exception.

We know from the chapter on the Carneddau that native ponies existed in Wales long before the Roman invasion. Fragments of harness and bit dated to the bronze age indicate a

**The Welsh Pony and Cob Society**
www.wpcs.uk.com

The A, B, C, and D represent the sections of The Welsh Pony and Cob Society stud-book. For all details except colour see in body of the text.

**Colours:** Any solid colour is acceptable but not piebald or skewbald. White socks and stockings are very popular, particularly in Sections A and B.

small equine probably 12hh or less. Naturally the ponies roamed across a large mountainous area and this helped create regional differences within the definition of 'mountain pony'.

The Welsh took their ponies and horses very seriously as far back as King Hywel Dda aka Hywel the Good (A.D. 942-948). He created laws

for north, south and south-eastern Wales – Venedotian, Dimentian and Gwentian respectively – which stated that no serf could sell a stallion without his Lord's permission. This also included a scale of pricing of ponies, which extended to their third year. A foal to a fortnight old, 4 pence; from fifteenth day to a year old, 24 pence; from a year and a day, 49 pence and at three years 60 pence. In the third year the animal would be broken to whichever work was intended. A riding pony was 120 pence worth but a working horse for cart or harrow a mere 60 pence. One entire stallion was worth three mares! The animal was also covered, within specific time limits, for a variety of diseases and behaviours. The buyer could return it for a refund if it proved to have staggers or was a weaver. Interestingly, a 'filly for common work' had a value on its tail, because in the Celtic lands, the harrow was traditionally harnessed to the tail.

In 1189 the historian Giraldus Cambrensis alias Gerald de Barri, Archdeacon of Brecon, wrote his famous 'Itinerary through Wales' and 'Description of Wales'. In Powys, south of Lake Bala, Gerald describes "most excellent studs put apart for breeding and deriving the origin from some fine Spanish horses, which Robert de Belesme, Count of Shrewsbury brought into this country." It would seem likely that this is one of the origins of the injection of foreign/Arab blood into the WMP and the starting point for the beauty of the ponies that we see today. The small head with a slightly 'dished' face seems such an obvious link to Barb blood and it is easy to see how a cross with a really good mountain pony could produce an animal of great quality.

# A. The Welsh Mountain Pony

**Height:** Not exceeding 12hh*.

**Characteristics:** The section A is the smallest of the four Welsh breeds. Intelligent, hardy, spirited, with a quick, free and straight action. Deep of girth and strong of leg, with a good slope to the shoulder and lean strong hindquarters, which help towards that archetypal springy gait. The dished face and refined muzzle, usually attributed to Arab influences in their history, combined with small ears but large eyes have meant they are generally considered to be the prettiest of all the native ponies.

*hands high is a unique measurement for horses. One hand is equal to 4 inches (10 cm).

The way that the ponies developed historically may explain why the current designations of the WPS are as complex as they are. In the Middle Ages there were three distinct types of horses/ponies in Wales; the palfrey, the rouncy (also sometimes rouncey or rounsey) and the sumpter. The first was a riding horse, more likely to be used by a lady. The rouncy was a great trotter and would be a squire's mount when he rode out beside his knight, who would be in full armour on a destrier (warhorse). The rouncy had to keep up with the destrier and act as a remount for the knight if the destrier fell in battle. There is a twelfth-century description by the Archbishop of Brecon of what were subsequently known as Welsh cobs as, 'Swift and generous steeds ridden into battle by the brave Welsh Princes and Chieftains against the invaders of their country.' The sumpter however, was very definitely just a pack horse.

There was also what was known as a working horse, a cob type, which if crossed with imported Andalusians could produce the legendary Powys Cob, which in turn became the Welsh cart horse, a cart horse but of moderately large pony size.

From the Middles Ages onward, the Welsh were keen to cross their equines to gain height, weight, smooth action and trotting ability; they were just keen on good ponies.

The WMP was always acknowledged to be the foundation stock for all later developments. It is interesting to note that, although quite distinct in appearance and perhaps more importantly height, there is definitely a familial likeness between the four current types. They all have the WMP character, poise, and tremendous dash and freedom of action.

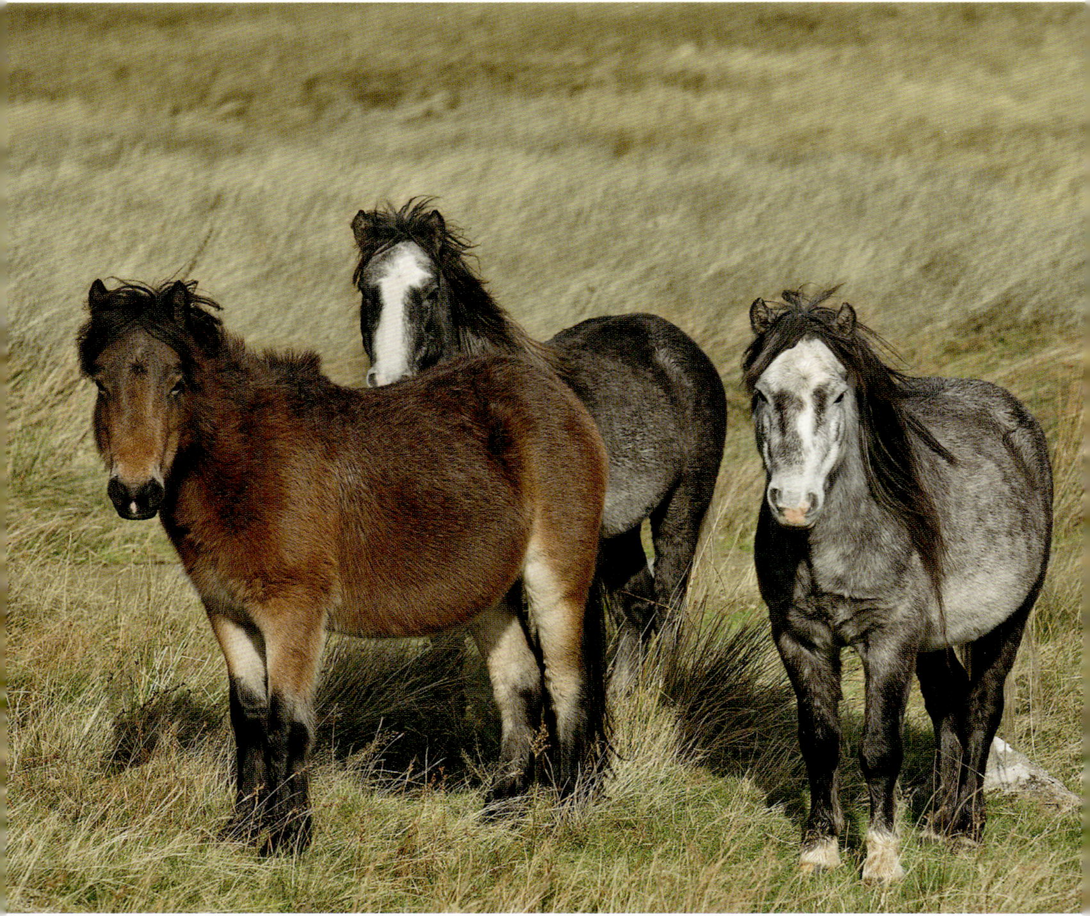

# B. The Welsh Pony

**Height:** Not exceeding 13.2hh*.

**Characteristics:** A larger pony than Section A. Often described as a riding pony with quality, hardiness of constitution but all with a strong pony character. An elegant and athletic ability of movement. There is a lightness of build, indicating thoroughbred or hackney blood in their past. There should be no loss of bone in the lightness and they should have a muscular arching neck.

*hands high is a unique measurement for horses. One hand is equal to 4 inches (10 cm).

It is easy to see how down the years, constant crossbreeding happened, just with the change of the seasons. Farmers who ran ponies on the mountains would bring them down to the homestead for the winter. The stallions of the herd would come with them and were not segregated from the solid working ponies in the yard/barn. Within a couple of years there would be a new strong, hardy pony working on the farm. The foundation breed however, has held true to type by the very nature of its environment – the poor grazing and a challenging climate.

# C. The Welsh Pony of Cob Type

**Height:** Not exceeding 13.2hh*.

**Characteristics:** The strength of the foundation stock Welsh Mountain pony but with cob blood. As always, active, surefooted and constitutionally hardy, with a gentle nature. The Section C is heavier and cob like with a compact close-coupled outline. There may be small amounts of feathering on the legs. Ideally suited for use by both adults and children, they have ability in both showjumping and competitive driving.

*hands high is a unique measurement for horses. One hand is equal to 4 inches (10 cm).

The cob type pony had to be the perfect all-rounder, able to run with hounds, pull a cart or a plough, and be ridden by a child. Before the instigation of a stud book, a stallion could be a goodly source of income for its owner. The stallion would be ridden or led from town to farm, hamlet to marketplace, to cover any mare offered up but at a cost. The Section B riding pony was traditionally produced from a Mountain mare and sired by a small quality cob. Then the hardy pony gained the size and strength of the cob.

The Welsh cob and the smaller but equally strong cob type were both heavily engaged in the 1914-18 war, as has been the case with other breeds in this book. Significantly this engagement was not just on the side of the British. It is documented that Germans visited Dalis Fair at Lampeter in 1914 and bought hundreds of 'light horses'. The cob gained a high reputation as what was known as a 'vanner': a pony for town traders, doctors and cabmen who all needed a strong, intelligent workhorse who would do well on a basic diet. Their versatility was perfect in agriculture too and the horse on a Welsh farm was often the pride of the farmer. It could also be a source of income, as the selling on of experienced horses/ponies at the end of spring sowing was a regular practice in rural areas.

The WMP was used in the collieries of Wales along with many other Mountain and Moorland breeds as mentioned in other chapters. There was however, no specialist stud to ensure the best WMP for the mines and, whilst the smallest were used fully underground, taller Welsh cob types were also used in the higher underground sections. The last colliery equine used underground was Robbie, who retired from the Pant y Gasseg mine near Pontypool in 1999.

The problems already described in these pages of ensuring that good quality stallions covered good quality mares meant that the ponies running the hills at the end of the 1800s were sadly neglected. Like Maske in the New Forest, there was one stallion who really left his mark. In the early part of the eighteenth century Merlin, a thoroughbred racehorse who had broken down on the track, was turned out on the Ruabon hills in Denbighshire. Very surprisingly, he seems not to have suffered from exposure in the open environment and raised considerably the quality of the stock in his area. Over time his offspring, 'Merlins' as they became known, reached higher prices at sales than other comparable ponies.

# D. The Welsh Cob

> **Height:** Not exceeding 13.2hh.
>
> **Characteristics:** A larger pony than Section A. Often described as a riding pony with quality, hardiness of constitution but all with a strong pony character. An elegant and athletic ability of movement. There is a lightness of build, indicating thoroughbred or hackney blood in their past. There should be no loss of bone in the lightness and they should have a muscular arching neck.
>
> *hands high is a unique measurement for horses. One hand is equal to 4 inches (10 cm).

Towards the end of the 1800s, two groups formed to try and raise the calibre of animals running on the Gower Commons, South Wales and the Longmynd Hills at Church Stretton, very close to the Welsh border. The Gower Union Pony Association and the Church Stretton Hill Pony Improvement Society both had the aim to 'encourage and assist the farmers to improve their often-neglected ponies'. Charles Coltman-Rogers, the Welsh agriculturalist, said of this endeavour, "On both these places the one-minded and far-seeing natives have had drifts of ponies, and ordered peremptorily off the scenes all that they did not wish to have about the place and messing around."

The first stud book containing Welsh ponies was created by the Polo and Riding Pony Society in 1898 (later the National Pony Society). The Welsh Pony and Cob Society was founded in 1901 and opened its own breed-specific stud book. The Commons Act (1908) made it legal to remove any entire stallions not of appropriate quality from

any common land and suddenly all eyes were on the mountain pony. Premium Shows, as already described in previous chapters began in 1913 and this put weight behind the improvement trend. It worked. It took time and effort to remove unsuitable colts and stallions from the hills and one association in Epynt in mid-Wales, even offered a reward of five shillings to any shepherd reporting an inappropriate animal. There were Associations/Societies that even bought their own stallions and charged 2/6 to allow a mare to run with them. Furthermore, to follow the lead taken by owners of other native ponies, breeders were barred from selling the offspring of premium stallions. The importance of mares began to be recognised and they started to be inspected and registered too.

Originally the Premium Show prizes had been £5 each but by 1916 they had become graduated £7, £5 and £3. Of the five granted that year: Longmynd, Gower, Black Mountain, Penybont, and Epynt, the Gower stallions were all of show standard. It is worth noting that the most favoured colours at this time were bay and brown. However, the effect of the outstanding stallion Dyoll Starlight was brought to bear and the colour most favoured for ponies of Section A and B became grey. Starlight was outstanding in the show ring, culminating in a Royal Show championship at the age of 20!

There were many studs and many stallions who stamped their qualities on the current Welsh Mountain pony. Although of different sizes and types, the WMP in the four forms we recognise today is well known throughout the world for its free-moving and spritely charm, and its excellence in all forms of equine sport. The perfect pony to cope with gymkhanas, show jumping, cross country, dressage and driving too. At the heart of all the ponies in all the sections is a kindly, intelligent, elegant animal who loves to work with humans and always gives of its best.

# The Rare Breeds Survival Trust

The Rare Breeds Survival Trust seemed a perfect fit to appear in this book as seven of the twelve pony breeds featured are on their watch list. Here is a statement about what they do, not just for horse and ponies but for cattle, sheep, pigs and other farm animals.

**Monitor:** They monitor the number of rare and native breeds. Every year they collect data from breed societies and use the number of animals registered in a year to estimate the total number of breeding females. From this they produce their annual Watchlist. They monitor threats to breeds. Other factors can threaten the breeds such as inbreeding and geographical concentration. They monitor and try to reduce these.

**Save:** They save genetics in the UK National Gene Bank. They collect genetics from animals, usually semen from males but also embryos. This is their insurance policy. If a breed were to become extinct, they can use this store to revive it. They save animals. In emergencies, RBST will buy genetically important stock and place it in approved breeding centres.

**Promote:** They promote the breeding and registration of rare and native breeds. Together their staff, members and support groups provide a network of knowledge to support and encourage breeders.

They promote the use of rare and native breeds for Food, Fibre and Conservation Grazing.

**Why they do what they do**
**Economic:** Increased diversity enables faster development of new traits. Native breeds provide a major contribution to our rural economy, both economic and culturally. There are around 30,000 herds and flocks of native breeds in the UK.

They contribute over £700 million to UK local economies.

**Social and cultural:** Native breeds are part of our national identity and heritage – and they represent a unique piece of the earth's biodiversity. They have inherited a rich variety of livestock breeds and their loss would impoverish agriculture and diminish the human spirit. We must work together, for the sake of future generations, to safeguard these treasures.

**Choice:** Today's consumer choices are increasingly influenced by environmental and welfare concerns and by tastes for speciality products. We must seize the opportunity this offers.

**Environment:** Grazing with native breeds plays an important role in the development and maintenance of natural habitats and increasing biodiversity.

**Risk reduction:** Genetic resistance is increasingly important for the control of animal diseases, today and in the future. Saving our native breeds can help us to face as yet unknown challenges in the form of disease resistance and susceptibility, climate adaptation, food security and resilience.

Growing global population and improvements in standards of living mean that there is a rapidly increasing demand for animal protein, with intensified animal production. This places increased risks and pressures on our natural resources, not least land and water. It is our task to protect our food and farming systems by maintaining secure alternative livestock genetic resources.

**Research:** There is still much to understand regarding nutrition, reproduction, disease resistance and susceptibility. Breed diversity will help research into these areas for both livestock and humans.

**www.rbst.org.uk**

Boy on white horse by Theodore Kittelsen.

# Myth and Legend

It would have been easy to include lots of horse myths and legends here but I was really keen to research just for ponies. The clue, as they say, is in the title of this book. This chapter therefore gives you a taster of the myriad tales that are out there. If you are particularly interested, you could follow the suggestions for further reading made by Pamela Thom-Rowe at the end of her piece on Mari Lwyd.

There is a shapeshifting water sprite throughout UK mythology which can sometimes take the form of a pony. The basic nature of the Brag/Braag (Northumberland) and the Ceffyl Dŵr (Wales) is much the same, with subtle variations. The end game is almost always that the human dies.

The Northumbrian variant has the rider, enticed by the pony to mount, then bucked off into a pond or bush. In Wales, the Ceffyl Dŵr, has the ability to fly and then just evaporates. The rider is then deposited from a great height. (The Scottish water-horse, the kelpie, has a similar *modus operandi* but is found around fast moving or secluded water.)

There is a far more dangerous variant of this type of tale, the sea and loch dwelling each-uisge in Scotland, (each-uisce in Ireland) which materialises as a horse, a pony or even a handsome man. In male form it is particularly fond of human women, who often prevail against the creature because of their quick wit. The each-uisge will, in any of its manifestations, work safely for a human but only inland. On catching scent or sight of water, its skin becomes sticky and it dives in to the lake or sea and drowns its rider. Rather gruesomely, it is said to eat the complete body of the victim, apart from the liver, which floats to the surface!

Running with the Stars. Stained glass by Tamsin Abbott.

Folklorist Pamela Thom-Rowe explains the roots and revival of the fascinating visitations of the Mari Lwyd.

## The Tradition of the Mari Lwyd by Pamela Thom-Rowe

There are many customs concerning horses and ponies in the British Isles but perhaps the strangest and most striking is that of the Mari Lwyd. The Mari Lwyd, or Grey Mare, is an old Welsh tradition performed at midwinter during the Twelve Days of Christmas. It consists of a horse or pony skull fixed upon a long pole and carried from under a large white sheet, sometimes decorated with ribbons. Traditionally the Mari would be led from house to house accompanied by a small party of men. At each stop the group would engage in poetic song and banter (Pwnco) to gain entry. If successful the company was rewarded with food and drink. This could be a noisy affair with music and song, the Mari a lively addition to the celebrations, her jaw

Above: Hannah Willow left and Tamsin Abbott right at the Mari Lwyd celebrations by Pamela Thom-Rowe.

Myth and Legend

Mari Lwyd by Hannah Willow.

snapping and cracking as she chased the occupants from room to room.

The occasion was accompanied by singing and requests for payment suggesting it was a type of wassailing to bring luck and good health. The earliest known record is from the late seventeenth century but there are older references to similar 'hooden animal' traditions. Early antiquarians believed it had ancient connections deriving from a pre-Christian past. Although there is no evidence of this, there is no doubt that the Mari Lwyd is associated with a time of seasonal change and re-birth. Her presence at the door facilitates our crossing over a threshold, from the cold outside to a warm inside and into an atmosphere of conviviality and celebration. The Mari Lwyd certainly has a liminal and mysterious presence but her origins remain obscure.

The Mari is now regarded by some as a symbol of the midwinter season and there has been a recent revival of the tradition. This is the coldest, darkest period of winter when folk get together to share food and high spirits. On certain occasions lively processions of men and women may be found walking beside wildly decorated Maris in proud celebration of the turning of the year.

Mari Lwyds are elusive and not easy to find. Perhaps you may encounter one at a wassail in the apple orchards of Wales and the Welsh Marches or in an unexpected moment in a village pub in quieter parts of the countryside. Wherever you find her it will be a memorable meeting!

Further reading:
*The Horse in Welsh Folklore: A Boundary Image in Custom and Narrative.*

*Juliette Wood in The Horse in Celtic Culture.*

*The Stations of the Sun Ronald Hutton.*

*The Customs and Traditions of Wales Trefor M. Owen.*

There is a very specific New Forest pony piece of folklore about a character called a colt pixie. Most often linked to the person of Robin Goodfellow or Puck, who is usually known as a rather benign character, although not in this instance. The colt pixie uses the guise of a little forest pony to lure humans and other animals to death in the forest's marshy bogs. There appears to be no actual tale behind this but it is recognised throughout the south west of England and there is a Cold Pixie's Cave barrow in the New Forest.

In the pagan calendar, Beltane May Day (1st May) has much significance for owners of ponies. On this day they would decorate birch branches with ribbons and hang them around the door of the stable, where they would stay for the whole year.

The birch offered protection against the ponies being 'hag-ridden' by witches. The birch is also connected in paganism to the fly agaric mushrooms which are often found at its base.

Right: The Protective Birch by Jenny Steer.

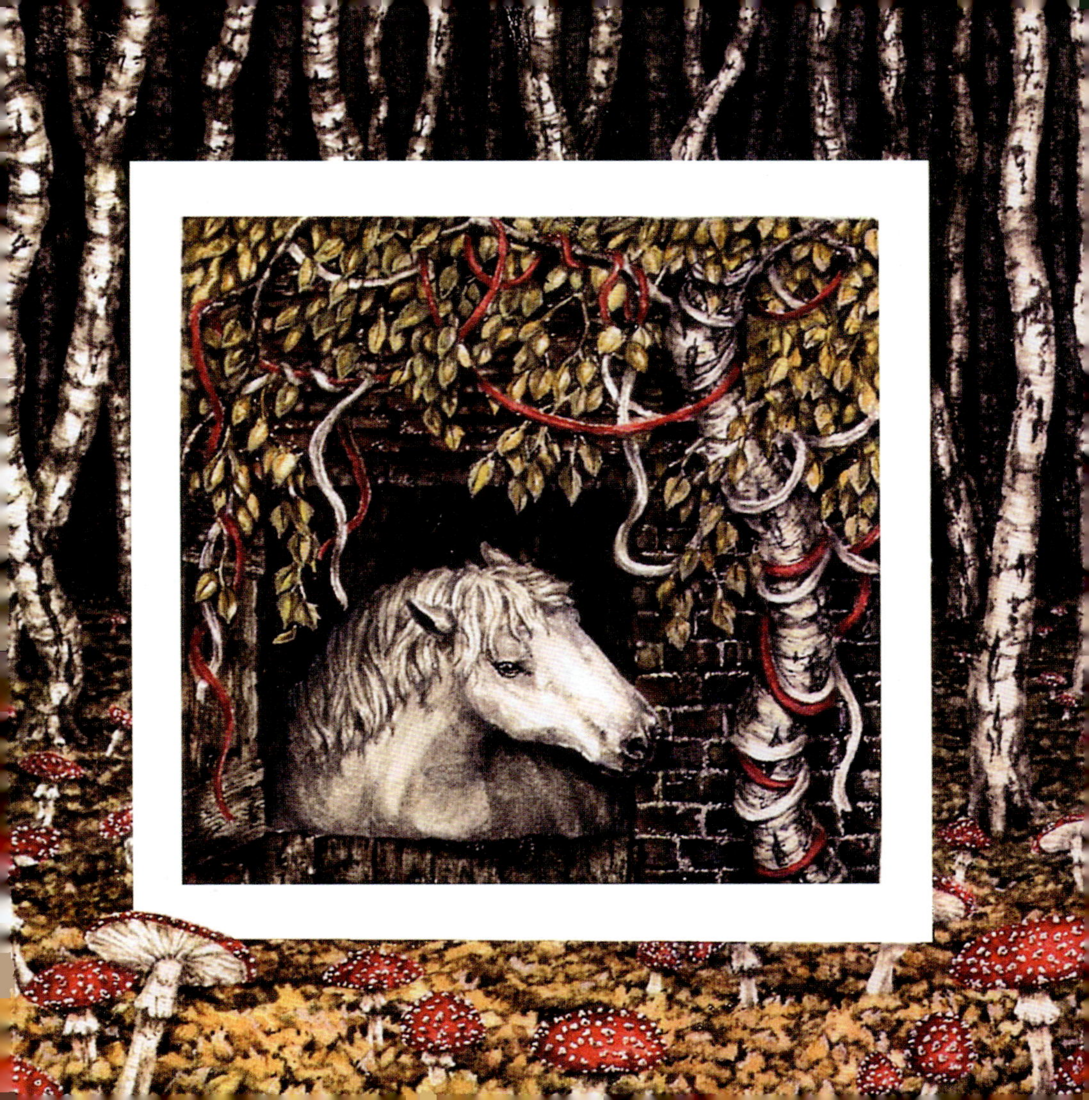

Leather journal by Skyravenwolf.

# Art and Literature

Unfortunately, the most well-known equine in literature is of course a horse. *Black Beauty* was written by Anna Sewell in 1877 and was the first novel written with an animal in the first person as an autobiography. It was an enormous success when first published and is thought to be one of the bestselling books of all time. Much copied for its clear message that life is a journey and kindness to animals and humans on the way is important to all.

Perhaps the first great pony in literature is *The Maltese Cat* in Rudyard Kipling's short story of the same name, published in the Pall Mall Gazette in 1895. (It was later published as a stand-alone book, illustrated by Lionel Edwards.)

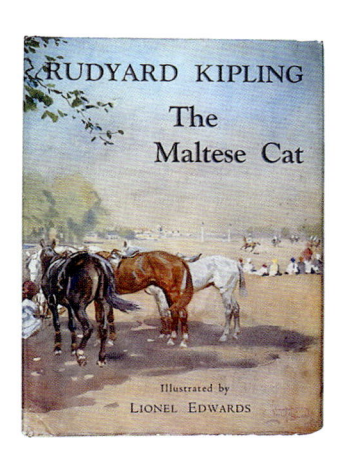

The story is told through the eyes of the ponies in a polo team. They are not just any team but are finalists in a polo championship, the 'Upper India Free for All Cup' taking place in north-west India in the 1880s. It is the ultimate fight of the underdogs, The Skidars a 'poor but honest native infantry regiment' with a limited number of ponies, against The Archangels from a British cavalry regiment, with a fresh pony for every chukka. The Cat is described as a flea-bitten grey, and says of himself that he was pulling a vegetable cart when he was spotted and taken to play polo, at which he excels. It is an exciting, funny and inciteful read and speaks of a time when equines were the centre of the world for everyone, high or low born.

*Moorland Mousie* by Golden Gorse (1929) tells, successive short stories, of the life of an Exmoor pony. It was recently reprinted to benefit the Exmoor Pony Centre; illustrations are by Lionel Edwards.

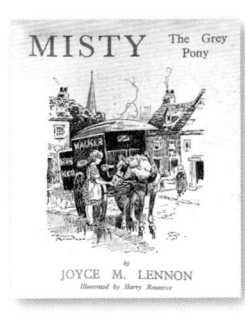

*Misty the Grey Pony* by Joyce M. Lennon, written in 1940, is a typical pony version of Black Beauty. It has the same story arc, with our heroine starting life in a stable with her mother and returning full circle many years later, having worked in a circus, pulled a milk float, and sometimes been treated badly on the way.

The 1920s saw the start of a slow increase in the teaching of riding to children, which by the mid 1930s was becoming a quiet obsession. The Princesses Elizabeth and Margaret both rode and perhaps this had something to do with it. The first proper 'pony books' are credited in the mid-1930s to Joanna Cannan, mother of the Pullein-Thompson pony writing clan. Josephine, Christine, and Diana Pullein-Thompson wrote their first pony book together in 1941 when they were just 15 and 14 (Christine and Diana were twins) and subsequently wrote over 100 between them. The books are well written and the pony knowledge deep, they may have been writing about it but they had all had the practical experience too.

There are one or two other significant writers of pony books from the 1950s. Ruby Ferguson wrote the much-loved Jill books, which started with *Jill's Gymkhana* in 1949. Jill is a feisty, funny character who has wonderful rather old fashioned adventures with her two ponies, Black Boy and Rapide in nine books written over twelve years. Pat Smyth, the international showjumper of the 1950s and 60s should also get a mention here with her Three Jays series. Whilst not having the writing quality of the Pullein-Thompsons or the personality of the Jill books, Smyth's tales, are workmanlike and factually interesting. Pat actually features in the books as a narrator following the exploits of her central characters Jackie, Jane and Jimmy and she incorporated huge amounts of useful horse information. They were wonderful for pony mad girls with little actual pony experience.

Although all the books of the 50s and 60s could be said to paint an idyllic Enid Blytonesque picture of life in the countryside and with ponies, they tapped into a need for a sense of security and a thread to follow in life. There are many more authors who filled this particular gap, Patricia Leitch wrote about the exploits of Jinny Manders in the 1960s and 70s. Her books set in Scotland, always gave a feeling that reflected her attitude to animal welfare and did not quite follow the middle-class framework of the previous writers. The love of ponies is still there in writers today, although nature, climate and the reality of life for most urban children does creep in.

Art and Literature    155

Cartoonist Norman Thelwell. © Thelwell Estate 2021, www.thelwell.org.uk.

No discussion of little girls and their fat hairy ponies is complete without a mention of the funny, evocative and knowing drawings of the wonderful cartoonist Norman Thelwell. His first 'pony and girl' cartoon was published in Punch in 1953. The response it generated was immediate and so began a lifetime relationship with her, her pony, her friends and their ponies, and her long-suffering family.

His first collection was published in 1957 under the title *Angels on Horseback* and the rest, as they say, is history. One of the standout characteristics of his pony work is that whilst being funny, he is never unkind. He appreciated both the ponies and the children and 60 years on, his art is still relevant and much loved.

## Sultan the Pit Pony

The Kelpies are a well-known Scottish landmark in Falkirk, depicting two enormous horse heads sitting on the ground. However, the pony has its own enormous landmark sculpture. Sultan the pit pony, can be found just over six miles north of Caerphilly at the site of the former Penallta Colliery, now known as Parc Penallta.

Designed by Welsh artist Mick Petts, the 200 metre-long-hill sculpture was created from 60,000 tonnes of coal shale. It is 15 metres high with stunning views across the created parkland to the countryside beyond. The project to use the site began in 1996 in a partnership between Caerphilly County Borough Council and Groundwork Wales. Mick Petts says of the work: *"During the development of Parc Penallta it was proposed to shelter the events arena from the prevailing winds with a bund of 60,000 tons of coal-shale, my role*

Sultan the Pit Pony by Mick Petts, Parc Penallta.

Art and Literature

*was to animate this landform into a recreational landscape & sculptural icon which symbolised the final release of the Pit-ponies onto the mountainside."* Although not named by the artist, locals named it 'Sultan' after a prize-winning pit pony who had worked at the pit.

There are walks and trails, cycle tracks and, appropriately, bridleways over Sultan and the whole site. Hoof-shaped pools on the hill brow fill with water and you can sit in the gazebo at his ear. Sultan is one of the largest figurative earth sculptures in the UK, a fitting exuberant monument to the many thousands of pit ponies that helped create the Industrial Revolution.

# Photo credits and artworks

Endpapers and page 1: Linocuts by Jane Russ.

Pages 7, 10–17, back cover 2nd from left: Carneddau, Allie Evans.

Pages 18–25: Connemara, Alan Piper.

Pages 26–37, back cover left: Dales, Jackie Snowdon.

Pages 38–47: Dartmoor, Lizzie Houghton.

Pages 48–55: Eriskay, Comann Each nan Eilean – The Eriskay Pony Society (CEnE).

Cover and pages 56–69: Exmoor, Trevor Clifford.

Pages 3, 70–81, back cover 3rd from left: Fell, Fleur Hallam.

Page 72 top left: Alamy.

Pages 82–90, 94–95: Highland 1, Melody Ashcroft, Heald Town Highland Pony Stud.

Pages 92–93: Highland 2, Ruaridh Fergusson.

Pages 83: Bassay Cross, Colin Park.

Pages 91: John Stewart-Murray, *Vanity Fair*.

Pages 116–127, back cover 4th from left: Shetland, June Brown.

Pages 96–103: Kerry Bog Pony, Kerry Bog Pony Society.

Pages 104–115: New Forest, Natasha Weyers.

Page 123: Ponies to mainland, *The Scotsman*.

Page 125: Jack 16, Gutenberg.

Pages 130–133: Welsh Mountain, Rhian Mai Hubbart.

Pages 128, 134: Welsh Mountain, Paul Stratford.

Pages 139–141: Section D Welsh Cob, Sian Broderick.

Pages 142–143: Rare Breeds Survival Trust.

Page 144: Public domain.

Page 146: Tamsin Abbott.

Page 147: Photo by Pamela Thom-Rowe.

Page 148: Hannah Willow.

Page 151: Jenny Steer.

Page 152: Skyravenwolf.

Page 153: Jane Russ.

Page 154: Jane Russ.

Page 155: Jane Russ.

Page 156: © Thelwell estate 2021, www.thelwell.org.uk.

Page 157–158: Photos by Paul Chapman.

Every effort has been made to trace copyright holders of material and acknowledge permission for this publication. The publisher apologises for any errors or omissions to rights holders and would be grateful for notification of credits and corrections that should be included in future reprints or editions of this book.

# Acknowledgements

This is the book I always wanted to write and it has, without a doubt, been the hardest. For each chapter a special thanks goes to the enormous amount of people who helped me by checking I'd got the details correct. For cross-reference, most things these days can be found on the net. However, nothing beats talking head to head with the people who have the inside track of knowledge. Therefore, I offer huge thanks and a big virtual hug to all those who supported this book. I could not have done it without your help and I am very, very grateful. Thank you to all of you. Every chapter had a supporter and I hope I have done your breed proud and it lives up to your expectations.

A very special thanks to all the fabulous photographers whose work appears here. It would be a much duller (and thinner) book without your contributions, so heartiest thanks go to you too.

Not only was this book challenging for me but also for the studio at Graffeg. A special thanks therefore to the wonderful Joana Rodrigues, she is a delight to work with and managed to keep calm under ever-changing parameters.

Finally, very many thanks to my chum Mary Pyne, who has done the first read through on every chapter and kept me in grammatical line. I have just one thing to say to you, Mary... hyphens!

The Native Pony Book
Published in Great Britain in 2021 by Graffeg Limited.

Written by Jane Russ copyright © 2021. Designed and produced by Graffeg Limited copyright © 2021.

Graffeg Limited, 24 Stradey Park Business Centre, Mwrwg Road, Llangennech, Llanelli, Carmarthenshire, SA14 8YP, Wales, UK. Tel: 01554 824000. www.graffeg.com.

Jane Russ is hereby identified as the author of this work in accordance with section 77 of the Copyrights, Designs and Patents Act 1988.

A CIP Catalogue record for this book is available from the British Library.

All rights reserved. No part of this publication may be reproduced, stored in a retrieval system or transmitted, in any form or by any means, electronic, mechanical, photocopying, recording or otherwise, without the prior permission of the publishers.

ISBN 9781913134822

1 2 3 4 5 6 7 8 9

**MIX**
Paper from responsible sources
FSC® C014138